Visions of the Spaewife:

A History & Practice of Fortune-Telling, Modern Practitioners in Scotland, and The Spaewife's Book

THE
VISIONS OF
SPAÉWIFE

The History & Practice of Fortune-telling,
Modern Practitioners in Scotland.
& The Spaewife's Book

ASH WILLIAM MILLS

Title: *The Spaewife; or, Universal FORTUNE-TELLER*
Digital Images: The National Library of Scotland- (L.C.2855(14)

Author: Unknown
Original Publisher:H. Crawfor, Bookseller
Date? 1827
Reprinted: Amazon KDP, 2021
Introduction/context: Ash William Mills©2021

Translation: Wikisource- *The Spaewife, or, Universal fortune-teller* (3245403)
Edited by Ash William Mills (2021)
Company: Scottish Cunning Ways Shop

Published by Scottish Cunning Ways

Acknowledgements

A BIG shout out to the people whose help and guidance allowed this book to come into existence. To **George Hares** (*The North English Witch*) for your constant encouragement and guidance with your wyrd ways of tarot. To **JD** (*Cunning As Folk*) for helping me understand the complicated arte of Astrology and introducing me to an animistic understanding of the planets. **Lisa Boswell** for your insight into Crysal Ball reading and fortune-telling in Romani culture. To **Susanne Swanston** (warriorchick13) - the most psychic person I know - for imparting unto me your otherworldly insight, as well as for being your fabulous self. To **Kelden Mercury** for doing a brilliant job in helping with editing and proofreading this book. To my sister and brother-in-law **Julie** and **Mark Jastresbski** for your constant support and unconditional love, and of course my sisters own natural abilities of Second Sight.

Index

**The History of Fortune-telling
in Scotland**   11

Fortune-Telling and the Law in
19th Century Scotland   13

Prediction-Making and
Fortune-Tellers in Scotland   15

The Spaewife Chapbook   18

Old and New Methods of
"Scryning" and Crystal Ball Gazing   22

Fortune-Telling of the Modern Age   27

Interviews From Modern
Professional Fortune-Tellers in Scotland   33

A Brief History on Chapbooks   49

The Spaewife; or, Universal Fortune-Teller   51

The Universal Fortune-teller; or
The True Book of Fate   107

Propitious and Unpropitious days to
undertake a project or event.   157

Are you born a king or a joker
Or the jack of all trades?
Are you the queen of someone's heart
What is the value of your face?

Are you here to dig for diamonds?
Well, bring along your spade
Seems that life is just a gamble
So just enjoy the game
When the dice you keep on rolling takes away what is your life
Don't give up, just try your luck, look a snake right in the eyes
Raise the stake and show some face, this round has just begun
If you think outside the box, there's no such thing as square one
Are you born a king or a joker
Or the jack of all trades?
Are you the queen of someone's heart
What is the value of your face?
Are you here to dig for diamonds?
Well, bring along your spade
Seems that life is just a gamble
So just enjoy the game
And if there's someone standing on your left-hand side, grab 'em
Tell them everything will be alright, tell 'em
If there's someone on your right-hand side, grab 'em
Tell them everything will be alright
'Cause no matter which sleeve you wear your heart
Whichever way you wear your crown
Tomorrow is another day, to turn it all around
I will, stop when I'm ready, I'll show everyone my cards
But for now I'll keep on playing
Even when the game gets hard

Lucy Spraggan, *Join the Club*

The History of Fortune-telling in Scotland

"*The Spae-wife of the Clachen*"—Painted by J. Phillop (1851)

Since my first book *The Black Book of Isobel Gowdie and other Scottish Spells & Charms* (2021) I have come to learn that the process of writing never goes quite how you intend and instead the book takes on a life of its own! I often refer to my book as my baby and in some ways, it is! The author births into the world a book, they give it a body (content), a name (title) and a cover (face), and then they leave the nest and go off into the world (publication). From then on, they sort of do their own thing, being loved by many people and met by many hands.

Originally this book was just going to be a reprint of the *The Spaewife: or, Universal Fortune-Teller* chapbook with illustrations of pages as well as the transcripts, which I did not include in my first book. However, I decided to include another chapbook titled; *The True Fortune Teller; or Universal Book of Fate* which was popular in Glasgow. My hope for this book is to bring awareness to the reader of the importance of treating today's fortune-tellers with the same respect they would anyone else in a skilled trade.

The Spaewife is an incredible chapbook on fortune-telling in the 19th century. Its popularity grew to such an extent that several editions were published in Scotland, first being published in Kilmarnock, and then in Edinburgh, Glasgow, and Falkirk. This fact indicates the growing interest in fortune-telling amongst the Scottish people during the 19th century. In fact, the term *Spaewife* is a title that is itself uniquely Scottish! Although rarely used today by the Scottish population, there are a few small communities that still use the term. I remember watching an episode of *Still Game* (filmed in Glasgow) where a Spaewife was reading in their local pub.

The word *Spae* comes from Old Norse *spá*, meaning to prophesize. In Scots the term spae or *Spey* refers to the act of prophecy as well as foretelling, predicting, or telling fortunes. For example, in Robert Burn's poem *Halloween* (1785) he writes that "[To] seek the foul thief onie place, For him to spae your fortune." Often different methods were used by people who practiced the Spaeing arts. For instance, Sir Walter Scott mentioned in his book *The Heart of Midlothian* (1818) that: "Spaeing folk's fortunes wi' egg-shells, and mutton-banes".

Although the term *spaeing folks* was sometimes used when referring to all genders, it seems, based on my research and recent conversations with local folks, that those who practiced the art of Spae were mostly women.

Spae is always used in a feminine sense, such as Spaewife or Speywivie (wivie referring to an elderly woman). You will not find Spae being used in a masculine sense, such as "Spae-laddie" or Spaehusband. However, this is not to say that only women can be spae-folk today, but that in the past it was primarily a woman's role within communities.

Astrology and predictions appeared to be a mostly male profession being that more men were allowed to attend higher education than women. Subjects such as alchemy, astronomy and medicine were practiced by learned "gentlemen" right up until the late 20th century.

Consider the painting at the beginning of this chapter, the *Spae-wife of the Clachen*, the British Museum describes the scene as:

> "A group of distressed people gathering before the hut of an old woman, sitting at the door at right with black cat at her feet and a horseshoe hanging over the entrance, through which a male figure is seen in the shadows."

Nothing much is known about the Spaewife of the Clachen other than her depiction in the painting. However, this painting portrays a Spaewife during 19th century Scotland as the typical fortune-teller or seer. Even the 1840-50's editions of *The Spaewife* chapbook included a woodcut showing a typical fortune-teller on the title page. Like many other magical practitioners during the 19th century, the role of cunning folk or fortune-teller would often be a side or second job for the working-class person. For those of the "lowest" class, this would have been their main source of income depending on the reputation that they held for their gifts within their community.

Spaewives were greatly reputed for having either some skill of divination or having the Second Sight. In the Gaelic regions of the West, there is the Gàidhlig term *taibhsear*, but this refers specifically to someone who has the Second Sight and sees visions. Additionally, the terms *ban-fhiosaiche* or *cailleach nam frìth* both refer to a female fortune-teller or seer. The latter, to be more specific, is an old woman who can perform the divinatory practice known as the *frìth,* which I will discuss in the next sub-chapter.

Fortune-Telling and the Law in 19th Century Scotland

The authorities in Britain have always been quite strict towards magical practitioners, especially in Scotland due to the Presbyterian Church which dominated the country. Although the Witchcraft Act of 1735 was repealed in 1951 (thanks in part to the efforts of occult figures such as Gerald Gardner and Cecil Williamson), there were still the odd few who were convicted during the 19th century. A newer act, known as the Vagrancy Act, was established in 1824 for dealing with street fortune-tellers and cunning folk. However, during the 19th and 20th centuries it was rare that someone would be convicted under this act unless they caused quite a stir amongst their community. The last person to be convicted in Scotland was the famed medium Helen Duncan (1897-1956).

Instead, the Vagrancy Act 1824 was put into place for dealing with street fortune-tellers and cunning folk. The Vagrancy Act of 1824 specifically targeted traveller communities, prostitutes, suspected witches, palmists and fortune-tellers, actors, artists, and beggars (including certain charity collectors). It was in section 4: Persons committing certain offences to be deemed rogues and vagabonds that referenced fortune-tellers, it states that:

> [F4] Every person pretending or professing to tell fortunes, or using any subtle craft, means, or device, by palmistry or otherwise, to deceive and impose on any of his Majesty's subjects.

Thus, during the 19th century, people on the streets of Scottish towns who offered services such as card reading, tea leaf reading, and palmistry were seen by the authorities as charlatans and vagabonds. Due in part to the age of enlightenment and the

industrial revolution, authorities no longer believed in or felt concerned about magic, superstition, and witchcraft. However, this did not stop some people from continuing to believe in such things and they would still seek advice from their local fortune-teller, charmer, or wise woman/man despite the laws against it.

Much of the population from all over Scotland still held "superstitious" ideas and morals. Often those who used or sought the means of predictions and divination would do so in private. For example, in the illustration (left) a Scottish palmist reads a person's hand behind a fence whilst others await their turn.

Although not as harsh as the punishment for those charged under the Vagrancy Act 1824 during the 17th century, those who faced this charge during the 19th faced up to a month's hard labour. Reoffenders, like Helen Duncan, could be imprisoned for a year.

That said, so long as they weren't causing much of a stir amongst the general public, the authorities would often turn a blind eye to the practices performed in the streets or in people's homes. Sometimes, even the authorities themselves would discreetly seek the services of a fortune-teller!

The Vagrancy Act 1824 remains in effect in England and Wales today. In Scotland, however, the act was repealed by the Civic Government in 1982. This means that in Scotland the law no longer discriminates against the homeless, street performers, or fortune-tellers. Perhaps the growing popularity of Fringe and other popular festivals in Scotland during the 1970's, which featured several street performers and fortune-tellers, may have been a contributing factor on the decision for its repeal.

With myself, and so many of my good friends working as diviners or fortune-tellers in Scotland for a full or part-time living, it makes me glad to be part of a country that is so liberal and compassionate towards people's profession regardless of whether the general public agrees with it or not!

Prediction-Making and Fortune-Tellers in Scotland

In the *gàidhealtachd* (gaeldom) the most popular form of divination was known as the *frìth* which involved omen-reading by means of specific ritual actions. It was the act of omen-reading by means of specific ritual actions. Specifically, the *cailleach nam frìth* or female diviner would walk around the house three times before walking over the threshold with eyes closed. Then the diviner would form a circle of their eye using their thumb and forefinger. Finally, opening their eyes, the diviner would interpret the first object they see as an omen. Other divinatory rites included Slinneanachd, which involved the interpretation of shapes found in the shoulder bones of mature sheep. There was also the necromantic rite of the taghairm which was used to receive knowledge of future events as well as advice.

There were also divination rites that were performed on special days of celebration such as *oidhche shamhna* (Samhuinn) or Halloween. On this night, divination practices were often focused on predicting one's future husband or wife. Robert Burns's poem *Halloween* mentions quite a few of the popular divination rites practiced on the eve of Halloween. Full details of these divination rites and practices are mentioned in detail in my book *The Black Book of Isobel Gowdie and other Scottish Spells & Charms*. A few more examples of divinationary rites include winning of the blue clew, pulling the stocks (kale or turnips), and sauty bannock.

Divination methods from the 19th century, many of which are mentioned in *The Spaewife*, that continue to be popular today include reading cards (cartomancy), palmistry (chiromancy), tea leaf/coffee ground reading (tasseography), and facial/body impressions (anthroposcopy). As coffee and tea began to be exported from the Eastern continent during the early 1600's, both drinks became popular in Britain. European importers and travelers who brought coffee and tea also brought along with them the Eastern divination traditions associated with them. The European game of playing cards with its Toledo pattern became the origins of tarot. Additionally, French and Italian immigrants brought with them their methods of divination too. Anyone who is familiar with playing cards will have heard of the nine of diamonds referred to as the "curse of Scotland." As Robin A. Crawford explains in his book *Cauld Blasts and Clishmaclavers* (2020):

> The nine of diamonds in a pack of playing cards. Various historical explanations have been offered, but the most common is that the design resembles the coat of arms of the Dalrymple family, which was associated with the Massacre of Glencoe, the union of the Parliament and anti-Jacobitism.

Recently there was some misunderstanding that tarot reading is a closed practice since it's often used by and associated with fortune-tellers and psychics amongst the travelling communities. This simply isn't true! Tarot, or shall I say fortune-telling by playing cards has been used by many Europeans from indigenous and non-minority cultures for many centuries now. I feel like I can't stress enough, as someone who is against people appropriating closed practices, that those supporting the same cause should do their research before spreading misinformation based on hearsay.

Back to the subject of popular divination, as these divination methods became a popular affair amongst the  working-class, importers, and travellers, it also became a great interest amongst the higher classes of society as a form of fun parlour games. For the higher class, fortune-telling was simply a means of entertainment rather than a profession as it was for the working class. I can imagine women at their tea parties saying, "*Oh, what does the book say about my hand Victoria?*" For the poorer folks of society, it would be their only source of income, and as they did so, no doubt playing up to people's stenotypes and fantastical ideas

During the early 20th century, more unusual methods of divination started to appear amongst street fortune-tellers and travellers in Scotland. For example, in 1900, the famous Romani fortune-teller of Edinburgh (right) would be seen on St. Giles Street using an unusual method of divination. To tell fortunes, she would have her African bird pick a ball, which represented one of the planets. Based on which ball was chosen by her bird, she would decipher the meaning for the client.

The Spaewife; or, Universal Fortune-Teller is not just useful for historians as a glimpse into the fortune-telling practices of 19th century Scotland, it can also be modernised for today's practitioners. I have personally modernised the divinationary

17

methods detailed in this chapbook and used them amongst friends and family.

The reason why divinatory chapbooks were so popular was because they appealed to people's interest in different movements at the time. Specifically, it appealed to romanticism due to the aspect of the travelling "Gypsy" being the descendants of the ancient Egyptians. These chapbooks also appealed to the Celtic revival as the Spaewife was viewed as being the bearer of the long-forgotten magic of the Gaels. Finally, the chapbooks appealed to spiritualism based on the idea of delivering one's own fate by otherworldly means. Books like the *Spaewife* became so popular because they touched on all the popular subjects of the era. Again, The Age of Enlightenment didn't stop people from believing in magic and destiny, many very much did especially amongst the working class. However, they were often looking at these subjects through a different lens such as a scientific one. Or, as was the case with books on palmistry, as the subject of strange curiosity and excitement. Thus, for the average Victorian, picking up a chapbook like the *Spaewife* would have definitely been an intriguing artefact to bring to a playing card night or tea party, or to have a go at reading your workmates palms, moles, or birth chart.

The Spaewife Chapbook

Before giving some historical context on how such a chapbook on fortune-telling became so popular during 19th century Scotland, I would firstly like to address its misleading and problematic title. One would think that the term "universal" meant that the practices of fortune-telling or divination noted in the chapbook would be common knowledge throughout Scotland, or even globally accepted and understood. But in fact, this just isn't true! One need only look at other chapbooks on the subject to see variations or differences in the fortune-telling practices of this century and to understand that the *Spaewife*'s title is very misleading, not just today but back when it was published as well.

During my research I came upon a wee book that was published a few decades before *The Spaewife* entitled *Mrs Briget's Universal Fortune-Teller*. I had been aware of other chapbooks within Britain, including one that was in circulation in Scotland, *The True Fortune-Teller or Universal Book of Fate* (Glasgow, 1840). This book, though, was more of an oracle book akin to *The Book of Answers* (1999) than something like the Spaewife. However, *The Universal Book of Fate* does have some fortune-telling methods using fingernails, which neither *The Spaewife* nor the *Universal Fortune-Teller* have. In comparing the texts, I was hoping to find many similarities, however I found that they only shared a few.

For example, *The Universal Fortune-Teller* contains basic information on astrology, whereas *The Spaewife* (despite stating it was written by an astrologer) has none at all! *The Spaewife* had information on divining a person by their physical features, known as *secret indications*, such as the position of moles, hair colour/type, shape of the nose or chin, etc whereas *The Universal Fortune-Teller* doesn't. Additionally, *The Universal Fortune-Teller* is lengthier and more complex than *The Spaewife*. The only similarity between both chapbooks is the interpretation of playing cards, but even then, the methods are different.

In the Universal Fortune-teller instructs the reader to use all the playing cards except for the Aces of the deck, where *The Spaewife* not only leaves out the Aces but cards 1-7 also to tell fortunes with. However, divinationary interpretations are the same when it comes to fortune-telling by Playing Cards. Is likely that *The Spaewife* detailed methods of fortune-telling, which was popular in Scotland at that time, but the author just simply filled in the caps regarding Playing Card reading by taking from the *Universal Fortune-teller*. So, similar in some ways but different in the rest. Not so a "Universal" fortune-telling practice as both authors would like to make out!

Being falsely portrayed or not, the *Spaewife* grew in popularity during mid-19th century Scotland, especially within the larger cities and regions. So much that several editions have been published over the decades. First being published for booksellers in Kilmarnock in 1827, then later in Glasgow, Falkirk, and

Edinburgh which you can see at the back of this book the illustrations of their title pages.

Now, whether the information on fortune-telling in the chapbook was taken from an actual Spaewife, is unknown. However, given the interest in fortune-telling at the time, it makes sense that booksellers would market the chapbook in this way to appeal to their customers. Either as a parlour game to the upper classes or a side-job by the working class.

In Scotland, many were fascinated by the mysterious figure of the Spaewife, as in England they were with the exotic "gypsy." At this time, both characters were romanticised with great fear, wonder and mystery. For the Spaewife it was as a bearer of ancient pagan knowledge regarding soothsaying or Second Sight. The "gypsies" were seen as the travelling people of ancient Egypt. However, we know now that none of this was true and was instead conjured up in people's minds due to ignorance, propaganda, and prejudice. For the bookseller, the fascination with these fantastical characters provided a great marketing strategy for selling their chapbook.

Although the stereotyped character of the Spaewife was enough of a draw for Scottish customers, those in England seemed to have needed more of an appeal. This is not to say that the English were more intelligent than the Scottish, but that the English had more of a taste for romanticism. *The Universal Fortune-Teller* had a backstory of "hidden knowledge" belonging to a so-called famous fortune-teller Mrs. Bridget or Mother

Mr Bridget the Norwood Gypsey

THE FAMOUS MOTHER SHIPTON
(Published as the Act directs by Samuel Baker Aug't 1797)

Bridget. She is described as a beggar and a "gypsy woman" who lived in Norwood, London. The editor had bought a few papers wrapped in cloth from an old gentleman, who said he had found them in Mother Bridget's hut. The editor described the manuscript, which had been written in unidentified characters and signs due to Mrs. Bridget not being able to read or write. Although, it is unclear as to how the editor was able to crack the code and translate it into English. Whether Mrs. Bridget existed or not, she surely bears a lot of similarities to another famous fortune-teller named Mother Shipton. Both have similar characteristics, physical appearances, and reputations. Putting aside the striking similarities between the lives and legends of Mother Shipton and Mother Bridget, when looking at the illustrations of these two women you might think they were the same person. Notice how both have a long chin and pointed nose, gesturing their finger upwards in caution or demand. Certainly, over the decades both characters have become blurred and blended into one another as they were used as a gimmick for marketing during the 19th century.

Old and New Methods of "Scrying" and Crystal Ball Gazing

I have practiced scrying and gazing for some years now. I remember the first time I knew that I could scry. I was 17 years old and a friend of mine, whom I met through a pagan moot (public meeting), showed me a round, flat piece of obsidian in a box covered in velvet cloth. It was then that I learned how to scry into objects with a dark reflection. I had heard from my mother and grandmother of travelling folks and fortune-tellers using crystals to receive visions. But this practice was simply known as *crystal gazing*. Although the methods used for scrying

John Dee's Scrying Mirror, *British Museum*

today might be modern and highly personalized, the practice itself is quite old. It was believed that gazing/scrying originated with people divining using bodies of water. In Gàidhlig culture there was the necromantic rite of *Taghairm*, in which a person seeking otherworldly insight would wrap themselves into a freshly skinned bull hide and sit beside a waterfall. Eventually, they would go into a trance-like sleep and communicate with spirits in order to receive knowledge of future events. Water sources have long been associated with the spirit world. Perhaps therefore so many precious artifacts belonging to ancient British cultures, which were given as offerings to ancestors, have been found in bodies of water. Scrying by gazing into dark, reflective surfaces has also been connected to the practice of looking into bowls of in or black-dyed water - a practice which is still used by today's diviners. Of course, this may have evolved into the use of dark coloured mirrors.

Often crystal balls would have been a very expensive and specialised object, which the working class of society couldn't afford. Even today, a decent quality crystal ball can be quite pricey. In the past, objects such as old fishing floats were used as a substitute, especially within wee fishing or harbour villages. Whenever I practice crystal gazing, I use a household light bulb that is no longer in use. These bulbs make perfect tools for as a spirit medium for crystal gazing because they are blessed by fire through the source of electricity. Additionally, the bulbs fit perfectly in the palm of your hand. You can also buy pearl light bulbs which have a hazier surface to them which can be useful in both scrying and crystal gazing. Also, if you don't wish to go through the effort of cleansing or recharging the bulb, you can discard it and use a new one once another bulb has gone out in your home!

Famous magical practitioners of the past would use dark objects to scry. For example, John Dee, who was an astrologer for Elizabeth I and founder of Enochian magic, used an obsidian mirror to receive visions from the angels. Today, Dee's mirror can be found in the British Museum, where I have had the pleasure of seeing it myself. The mirror's wooden case is covered in tooled leather. Sometime during the 17th-century, art historian Horace Walpole added a handwritten quote from Samuel Butler's poem "Hudibras" which goes:

> Kelly did all his feats upon
> The Devil's Looking Glass, a stone;
> Where playing with him at Bo-peep,
> He solv'd all problems ne'er so deep

It has been said that Dee's companion in the magical arts, Edward Kelley, was the primary one who used the mirror to communicate with angels. Kelley did this in order to retrieve hidden knowledge from the angels while Dee recorded his insights.

In a modern Scottish context, there is the so-called *keek stane* mentioned in Raymond Buckland's book *Scottish Witchcraft: The History and Magick of the Picts* (1991) claims it to be a Scot's word for a scrying stone. However, I am unable to find reference to this stone anywhere else within Scottish folklore. Other than that, I have been informed by other Scottish folks that these divinatory devices were simply known as "reading crystals." The act of scrying itself was referred to as "looking into the crystal ball." Additionally, it was common for a fortune-teller to ask the client to touch the crystal ball, either for luck or to create a better connection. From what I gather crystal ball gazing and scrying are totally different forms of divination. The crystal ball acts as an energy or spirit vessel which aids a psychic, or person with the second sight, to focus. This allows them to receive visions internally, as opposed to seeing images or figures within the crystal ball like wgar can be done with a dark reflective surface. The crystal ball can also act as a meditative tool, facilitating a trance state during which intuition can flow freely to divine for someone.

When I was young, I learned about scrying using a darkened glass or crystal while reading books on modern witchcraft, Wicca, and paganism. Although I found that I had a natural ability, it was by speaking to other magical practitioners that I learned how to perfect my art. Eve, a good friend of mine and a well-respected person within the pagan and magical community, who recently passed away, taught me to use a dark room or black shroud and a lit candle. She told me to relax my gaze while focusing on a black mirror and to allow images and shapes to come to me upon its surface. As mentioned before, scrying is a skill which takes a lot of patience and practice to master and do at will. After 17 years, I am able to scry as well as I can perform any other form of divination. I even have my own method for preparing and using a scrying device, which I will share after giving a historical example.

The manner of making the Mirror of Solomon, useful for all divinations - *Grimorium Verum* (1817)

In the name of the Lord, Amen. YE shall see in this mirror anything which you may desire. In the name of the Lord who is blessed, in the name of the Lord, Amen. Firstly, you shall abstain from all actions of the flesh, and also from any sin, whether in word or action, during the period of time laid down herein. Secondly, you must perform acts of good and piety. Thirdly, take a plate of finest steel, burnished and slightly curved, and with the blood of a white pigeon write upon it, at the four corners, these names:
JEHOVA, ELOYM, METATRON, ADONAY.

Place the steel in a clean, white cloth. Look for the new Moon, in the first hour after the Sun has set, and when you see it, go to a window, look devoutly towards Heaven, and say: O Eternal, O King Eternal! God Ineffable! Thou, who hast created all things for the love of men, and by a concealed decision for the wellbeing of man, deign Thou to look on me, N., who am Thy most unfit and unworthy Servant, and look upon this, which is my intention.

Deign to send unto me Thine Angel, Anael upon this same mirror; he does command and order his companions whom Thou hast formed, O Most Powerful Lord, who hast always been, who art, and who shall ever be, so that in Thy name they may work and act with equity, giving me knowledge in everything that I shall seek to know of them.

Now you are to throw down upon the burning embers a perfume. While you are doing this, say:

In this and with this, that I pour forth before Thy face, O God, my God, Thou who art blessed, Three in One, and in the state of exaltation most sublime, who sits above the Cherubim and Seraphim, who will judge the earth by fire, hear me!

This is to be said three times. When you have done so, breathe three times upon the surface of the mirror and say:

Come, Anael, come: and let it be thy agreement to be with me willingly: in the name + of the Father, the Most Puissant, in the name + of the Son, Most Wise, in the name + of the Holy Spirit, the Most Living!

Come, Anael, in the terrific name of Jehova! Come, Anael, by the power of the everliving Elohim! Come, thee, by the right arm of the mighty Metatron!

Come to me, N., and order thy subjects so that they may make known to me through their love, joy and peace, the things that are hidden from my eyes.

When you have finished this, raise your eyes toward Heaven and say:

O most powerful Lord, who does cause all things to move in accordance with Thy will, listen to my prayer, and may my intentions be agreeable to Thee! O Lord, if it be Thy will, deign to gaze upon this mirror and sanctify it, that Thy Servant Anael may come thereto with his companions, and be agreeable to me, N., Thy poor and humble servant! O God, blessed and raised above all the spirits of Heaven, Thou who livest and reignest for all time. Amen.

When this is done, make the Sign of the Cross over yourself, and also on the mirror on the first day, and also on the next forty and five days. At the end of this time, the angel Anael will appear to you, like unto a beautiful child. He will greet you, and will order his companions to obey you.

It does not always require as long as this to cause the angel to appear, however. He may come on the fourteenth day, but this will depend upon the degree of application and fervor of the operator.

When he comes, ask him whatever you may desire, and also beg him to come and do your will whenever you shall call him.

When you want Anael to come again, after the first time, all you have to do is to perfume the mirror, and say these words: Come, Anael, come, and let it be thy agreement --and the rest of this prayer to Anael as we have given you above, until the Amen.

Dismissing the Spirit

When he has answered your questions, and you are satisfied with him, you must send him away by saying this:

I thank thee, Anael, for having appeared and having fulfilled my requests. Thou mayest therefore depart in peace, and shall return when I call unto thee.

The perfume of Anael is saffron.

Note: The spiritual being worked with in this ritual; Anael is the angel who resides over Venus, and is a spirit described to be a beautiful youth that is female, male, or sometimes both!

To Prepare a Scrying Mirror, Stone, or Crystal Ball
by Ash William Mills

Before the night of a dark moon, prepare a blend of Mullein, Eyebright, and Wormwood. Mix these herbs while calling on your ancestors, or a deity from your tradition or culture who is associated with divination. For example, those whose practices are Irish in flavor may wish to call upon Ogma (Ogham), Brigid (augury), or Dalan (stave throwing) for assistance in divining. Additionally, while placing each herb in your mixing bowl, as the spirit of each plant to aid you in blessing your scrying device as an object to connect the living and dead.

Wash your scrying object with either holy or well water while saying:

I clean and cleanse you (object) of all previous past associations or negative afflictions. Be now a tool for my desire to peer into the Otherworld of spirits and to receive visions from you.

You may want to give your scrying device a name. If so, you can give it life while blowing three breaths upon its surface, sprinkle the device with water three times, and say:

I bless you [name] in the name of the three (i.e The father, son and Holy Spirit, or Earth, Sea and Sky etc)
To obey me in time of foresight, divining and visions,
Be thee hollowed, consecrated and blessed!

The next day, just before twilight, take the scrying device to a graveyard - even better if your own family has been buried there. Give offerings to the grim spirit who guards the graveyard and begin walking until you are spirit-led to a particular grave or place in the yard. Make an offering to the spirit of the grave, asking them to bless your scrying device with the hole big enough to put your device in and place it a hole made in the soil, stating your intentions again to the spirits of the Graveyard. Before covering it up with soil, place upon your scrying device the herbal mixture along with three crow feathers. Focus on the object and then, closing your eyes, visualise a dark blue light radiating around your scrying device. Then open your eyes and say with strong benediction:

Fiat! Fiat! FIAT!

After you have buried your scrying device you might want to pour a little Holy water or water from a sacred Well over it in the name of the Trinity. Then walk away without looking back. After seven days you may return to the graveyard and retrieve your scrying device. On the next full moon, take your scrying device to a window. Holding it up to the moon's reflection say:

Moon light, moon shine bright,
Give onto this [name] the gift of sight.
So be it!

Moving forward, I would advise you to bond with the scrying device. Perhaps try to scry into it that very night. Additionally, learn how to work with your device by communing with its spirit and power.

Fortune-Telling of the Modern Age

My mum told me that when she was pregnant with me, she was randomly approached by an Irish traveller who told her that I would be born "gifted." In some ways I guess the traveller was right as I'm a bit of a jack o' all trades. The traveller asked for no money and was gone as soon as my mum looked back.

Today, professional fortune-tellers work the skills in many ways than were done in the past. Some provide services at home through online platforms, while others do so at pub events. There are also those who continue to work out of the traditional tend, wagon, or street stall. Even the idea of "crossing the hand with silver" has changed with payments now being often made through bank transfer or PayPal. Methods for divination are also a lot more varied today, with tarot and oracle decks being more popular than ever before. You only need to go into an Esoteric shop to see just how many different divination cards are available today. The deck that I use is the Connolly Tarot, which was given to me by my dad before he passed away. Now, every time I use this deck for a reading, I call upon my dad from the spirit world for assistance in divining. Recently, I have also started to read with Lenormand cards as well.

Funny enough, when I was searching for the right deck, I looked at deck upon deck on the internet for one that stood out to me but to no avail. I failed to find one that suited me. A week later, without having previously mentioned my search, my dad presented me with a deck that he bought from a carboot sale. I was delighted as the imagery and style of the deck was just what I had in mind. My point here is that there are so many decks to choose from that it can be very overwhelming. However, the variety also means that the fortune-teller can find a specific deck that calls to them!

Fortune-telling became much more popular during the early 19th and 20st centuries. Many companies responded to peoples' increased interest by starting to manufacture divination items including fortune-telling playing cards (such as the Lenormand), tea leaf reading cups, and even crystal balls. However, many of these fortune-telling methods saw a decline over time. For example, tea leaf reading became less popular after tea bags were introduced by Tetley Tea and other companies. Additionally, the use of regular playing cards for divination was soon overshadowed using tarot cards. The most available tarot deck to the public during the early 1900's, and one that remains popular today, was the Rider Waite which was illustrated by the unrecognised artist Pamela Colman Smith.

Today, there are several modern methods for divination based on ancient forms, such as Ogham, runes, casting of lots/bones, and scrying. There are also completely modern methods, such as the Witches' Runes that I have seen. It's strange because we know in the past, fortune-tellers would use crystal balls and show stones to see into the past, present, and future. Yet, in my research I found little mention of these techniques in the chapbooks of the 19th century.

Another reason why crystal-ball gazing may have been less frequent was the fact that the crystal itself was likely expensive and difficult for many people to obtain. However, I have read of people in the past using old or broken fishing floats for the purpose of gazing. Today, it is quite popular with folk magicians or witches to use these fishing floats. I have one hanging up in my living room window. However, I can't really recall a time where I have used my fishing float for scrying. Instead, I have previously used a dark mirror (made by spray painting the glass in a picture frame) and a flat piece of obsidian given to me by a past partner. It's the only time I would use a crystal due to the unethical ways they are sourced! I currently use a beautiful antique glass bowl which came with a pouring beaker decorated with thistles and shamrocks. Everything about it calls out Scottish Cunning craft to me!

Besides tarot, additional forms of divination that I have used for over 7 years now include *flipping the coin* and what is known as *casting the lots* (in some cultures this is known as *casting the bones*). Which method I use depends on what I'm divining about. If I want to ask the spirits a straight yes or no question, then I flip the coin. I do this by placing two coins over the eye sockets of a skull tea light holder (previous photo). This represents the old funeral custom of *paying the ferryman*. I ask my ancestors to aid me in my divining before taking the coins and throwing them down. If both coins land heads-up the answer is yes, if one lands tails-up it's a no, and if both land tails-up the answer is unknown and to try again later.

Author's ancestor divining skull and coins (5p's) as explained in text.

The Authors black glass Scrying bowl and pecker, circa 1960-1970's

When casting the lots, which is a popular form of divination within the Hoodoo and Conjure traditions of North America, I throw certain objects down upon a symbol or marked cloth. Interpretations are then divined based on where each object lands. I prefer to use everyday objects when casting lots, including keys, coins, dice, jewellery, and even bits of bone. The way I cast lots involves placing my objects into a small cup, asking ancestral spirits (either my own of those of a client) for help, shaking the cup three times, and then emptying the objects out all at once upon my casting cloth. There are some good books out there on how you can cast and interpret lots, such as Mama Starr Casas's *Divination Conjure Stye: Reading Cards, Throwing Bone, and Other Forms of Household Fortune-telling* (2019). However, I have my own method, which I sell on my Etsy store *Scottish Cunning Ways Shop*. An example of how I read when casting lots is as follows. If a coin lands on the briefcase symbol (which represents work or business) but a bone (which represents the client) land on the downward arrow (which represents decrease), this means that money is flowing nicely but your spending habits need to be kept in check.

There are some forms of fortune-telling that are not as popular today, including reading coffee or tea leaves. Tea parties, or high tea as it is known today, was very popular among the higher class during the 19th century and later the working class in the 20th century. My own grandmother and great aunt used to read tea leaves every time they had big social gatherings at their homes. They both used to get out their "good China" to impress their friends, which was a luxury for most working class at this time. Oftentimes, the good China set was only used on wedding days or special anniversaries, as it was for both my grandmother and great aunt. Although I never met my grandmother (despite sharing a birthday) to learn the "old family ways" such as tea leaf reading, I did learn a few things from my great aunt when I was a young bairn. To look at, my great aunt could be quite scary as she had what we call today "resting bitch face" and a cloudy-like eye from having cataracts in her younger years. But truly, she had a heart of gold and was one of the nicest people I have known. Every time we visited, she would have a spread out on a wee table of lemonade, custard cream biscuits, caramel wafers, and such. Much of what I know about my grandmother comes from my great aunt Nora, as they were best friends.

I have found that I carry the same natural ability as my grandmother and great aunt to interpret the shapes and figures of tea leaves. I feel great knowing that I am the only one in my family to carry on this practice. I read tea leaves using the same bone China tea set that was given to my grandmother as a wedding gift by her friends. The China set is decorated with one of my favourite wildflowers, Herb Robert. I only acquired one singular cup and saucer of this precious set after persuading my dad, who told me I would have the complete set after he passes. Now that he is peacefully in the spirit world I have the full set, which I treasure dearly.

Although I am aware that there are some charlatans in the towns of Scotland, there are many more well-respected fortune tellers who are very passionate and skilled in what they do. In the modern world, where people tend to be more sceptical or spiritual than religious, I find it a positive thing that these arts are finally being seen as a respectable profession. Some of my good friends, who are professional fortune-tellers, are also finding that people are starting to have more positive attitudes towards divination.

Interviews from Modern professional fortune-tellers in Scotland

Here I have included written interviews of modern professional fortune-tellers in Scotland for the reader to get a susceptive of what life is like to be reader in today's world. I feel, like many researchers and folklorist of the past, this kind of fieldwork is fundamental in compiling together up-to-date information of the practices and work involved in being a professional fortune-teller today. The interviews collected here are from reputable fortune-tellers working within Scotland and reflect true accounts of the practices of divination and the fortune-teller, and how they are approached by or work with clients today. I am pleased to present fortune-tellers: George Hares (Tarot), J. D. Kelley (Astrology) and Lisa Boswell (Crystal Gazing/Tarot).

Name: George Hares

Name of Business: George Hares/Bucca Botanica

Location in Scotland: Glasgow

Q. What is your main form of divination used as a professional fortune-teller?

A: Tarot all the way! In particular the Raider waite deck.

Q. How long have you been doing it for?

A: I've been reading the tarot since I was 11 years old, I'm 32 now which means it'll be over 20 years I've been reading tarot cards for people all over the world which I absolutely love.

Q. Do you have any previous connections with fortune-telling i.e family, friends etc?

A: My mum is a clairvoyant and a spiritualist, so the practice of spiritualism and spiritualist churches are something that I've grown up with and have very fond memories of, my cousin also used oracle cards in particular the faery oracle based off the artwork of Brian Fraud which I always loved.

Q. *How do you think professional fortune-telling has changed compared to the past?*

A: I think now that other forms of divination that are different from tarot card reading is still prevalent but sadly decreasing. An example would be a fortune teller in Edinburgh that used to perform readings with birds that she kept in a cage. Whilst I'm against caging animals, I find the different ways people performed readings was much more varied then back in the day and that aspect of divination interests me greatly. Another example is that cunning folk dripping hot molten lead through keyholes again forms of divination back then were more varied, whereas today tarot cards as much as I love them, have major dominion over readings today than they did in the past. Another aspect is some people nowadays can have very unrealistic ideas of what a reading can actually entail, I don't know the cause of this, but I know there seems to be a growing attitude of people wanting to hear what THEY want to hear and ignoring advice rather than what actually is.

Q. *what book would you recommend in learning your favoured fortune-telling?*

A: I have a confession. Having been reading tarot for over 23 years, I haven't read a full book on tarot, just the meanings at most. A lot of the time it has been self-taught, I watched my mum and her friends doing their tarot nights and listened to what the cards meant as a kid. When first properly starting out at 11 I read them psychically as in what the images told me rather than what a book told me, however that being said I also learnt them traditionally. In a pack of tarot cards particularly within the Raider waite, you get a booklet that the cards come with. Every night before I went to bed, I took a single card out and read the traditional meanings then went to sleep with them underneath my pillow and in the morning read the meanings whilst spending the day pondering on the meanings of the card, that's how I learnt the traditional way.

Q. *where can we find you for your fortune-telling services?*

A: YouTube: *George Hares*

Instagram: *thenorthenglishwitch*

Etsy: *Bucca botanica*

Name: JD Kelley

Name of Business: *Cunning as Folk*

Location in Scotland: Edinburgh & Largs

Q. *What is your main form of divination used as a professional fortune-teller?*

A: Astrology

Q. *How long have you been doing it for?*

A: In one form or another for over 20 years.

Q. *Do you have any previous connections with fortune-telling i.e family, friends etc?*

A: I made friends with folks much older than me when I was younger and several of the people that were playing with divination became very close friends.

Q. *How do you think professional fortune-telling has changed compared to the past?*

A: In recent times, more generally, I would say that three things which have muddied the water: lack of staying with the context of the query, overly psychological framing, and the need to render everything 'positively'. This can be the case in both modern cartomancy and modern astrology. I'm all for the flexibility of the symbolic—I am a huge fan of elasticity. However, I think folks come to a fortune teller for clarity, not a lecture on what something 'means' or to have their hand held as if they cannot hear difficult news. As the relationship between the querent and fortune teller is one based on trust, we owe it to them to give it clearly and kindly. Specifically, to astrology, a particular aspect that I think is important to raise is the complete lack of familiarity many modern astrologers have with the actual observational dynamics of earth and heaven. There is a focus on the 'map' of the chart and no awareness of what it speaks to.

Q. *What book would you recommend in learning your favoured fortune-telling?*

A: Effective practice comes from method. If you have the right method, you can divine with anything. A truth attested to by the many ways that we approach this art. I would recommend accessing teachings on method. The books *Traditional Astrology Course: Essential Concepts & Interpretation Basics* and *On the Heavenly Spheres* by Avelar and Ribeiro give an incredible foundation and very clear practises for delineation. When it comes to the deep knowledge of the dynamics of earth and heaven, there is, of yet, no text that will ever compare to spending time observing. I would suggest becoming very interested in observational astronomy as part of one's foundational learning in astrology. The language is emerging from these dynamics.

Q. *where can we find you for your fortune-telling services?*

A: You can find me at cunningasfolk.com where I teach and practice my occult and interpretive arts, or you can follow me on all channels @cunningasfolk.

Name: Lisa Boswell

Name of Business: *Divination and Fortune Telling*

Location in Scotland: West Lothian

Q. *What is your main form of divination used as a professional fortune-teller:*

A: Over the years, I have learned many systems of divination but my favourite by far is Lenormand cards. Lenormand is a 36-card system with images that are based on items you often come across in your day-to-day life. For example, there is a Fox card, a Clover card, an Anchor card, and so on.

I like Lenormand because I specialise in teaching predictive divination and Lenormand is easy to use for prediction. Lenormand cards are read in something known as a Grand Tableau spread. The Grand Tableau covers everything you would ever want to know including finances, love, enemies, even letters you might receive in the future! You can make these predictions without knowing anything about your seeker, so Lenormand is ideal for professional readers.

Q. *How long have you been doing it for?*

A: I started reading Lenormand back in 2014. I have been practicing fortune telling for pretty much my entire life and I began reading Tarot at the age of 7. Tarot used to be my 'go-to' divination method.

However, when I was 24, I was performing a professional reading and my Tarot cards magically stopped working for me! I soon realised that other methods I know (such as crystal ball reading) were also now impossible to connect to.

Back then, I performed readings for a living, so I obviously needed to fix the problem super quick. That's when I conducted some research and discovered Lenormand.

Q. *Do you have any previous connections with fortune-telling i.e family, friends etc*

A: Yes, I am Romany Gypsy and, historically, my family have been quite well-known fortune tellers. The infamous witch, Granny Boswell, was my great-great grandad's sister.

Growing up, my great grandparents lived in the yard next to the house where me and my sister's lived. We used to hear about how she and her daughters had read members of the royal family or actors and actresses.

My older sister used to watch some of the TV programs which featured the actresses my great granny and aunts had read for. I think this was partly one of the reasons why she developed an interest in fortune telling – she told my mum that she wanted to practice divination and my mum purchased a Tarot deck for her. Eventually, I started to use it and my mum gifted me my first deck also.

It is not as common for Gypsies to read Tarot as it is for us to interpret dreams, read tealeaves, or use crystal balls. I've always been big on tradition, so I also learned these systems as a child.

I was certainly influenced by my family, but I have a natural love of divination. I think if I would have been born into a different family, I would have had the same interests.

Other than that, my sister's best friend, Derek is a pagan witch and Scottish diviner. It was good growing up with someone outside of my culture because we could share ideas, discuss correspondences, talk through dream symbolism, etc. I think all readers should have someone outside their own little bubble who can help them to develop as a diviner.

Q. *How do you think professional fortune-telling has changed compared to the past?*

A: Around 10 years ago, there was a push by a lot of (very vocal) readers to reject prediction. Holistic and self-help centred divination was in and predictive fortune telling was out. There was a move towards repositioning Tarot and Astrology as something practiced by the educated middle and upper classes, similar to what happened with Yoga back in the '90s.

In Facebook groups and online forums, there was this air that only well-educated readers should become divination teachers. I had been told several times that I should go to university and get a degree otherwise I would not be respected in the right 'circles.' It is crazy to think that there are people who think that way, but there are.

Back then, people would brand themselves as 'enlightened, elite, intelligent' and predictive readers as just stupid. As a predictive reader, this trend affected me. I used to receive emails from other Tarot readers which said that I was, "Putting Tarot back 150 years."

Now-a-days, people care more about your experience in actually teaching and performing readings. Potential students are a lot less likely to learn from you just because you have a degree in an unrelated subject. Students want you to prove through your online platform that you have what it takes to provide them with what they need in a teacher. That don't really care about anything else.

I think this change is down to the civil rights movement. It is no longer fashionable to attack someone like me for my cultural beliefs because doing so looks racist and classist.

Plus, people are now discovering online groups and forums at the very start of their journey before they're influenced by anyone else. Newbies are clear on why they would like to learn divination whether it is so that they can predict the future of their relationships, careers, etc. For that reason, they are very honest with what they want from their fortune telling journey.

Q. What book would you recommend in learning your favoured fortune-telling?

A: To be honest, I have never read a divination book I liked.

Q. *Where can we find you for your fortune-telling services?*

A: I no longer read for the public as I teach divination full time. If you would like to learn from me, you can find my courses, e-books, and other trainings at www.divinationandfortunetelling.com

Conclusion to the Interviews

Knowing each of these people myself and spoken to them personally regards to the subject of fortune-telling and their trades in that aspect as a professional reader it is nice to see to read their options get out in an interview and see fortune-telling from each of their susceptive. In each interview I am see similar themes and good points regards in being a professional fortune-teller today. One main thing being which stands out is the respect (or shall I say, lack of) that the fortune-teller receives from clients or enquirers. They all seem to make a point that today people expect way more than they should off a reader and have unrealistic ideas in what they think a readings outcome should be. Myself, and persons interviewed as witness rather rude and daunting statements from clients like "prove you're a psychic?" or "can you give me a free taster reading to see if your genuine!". Which I feel in the past would not have come out of the mouths of enquiring clients. Fortune-tellers were respect or feared, or both, and would be approached with awe and politeness of their services they were willing to impart their wisdom and magical insight of the past, present and future of the client. To which I must stress to the client seeking a fortune-teller today to please be respectful and treat them with the same respect you would your plumber, electrician, or builder, they all have a trade which is just as valid and useful for the community.

Also, which most of the readers in this interview having over 20 years' experience or having a family background in fortune-telling or spiritualism, that should be more than enough to store your confidence in that fortune-teller. Not to mention the experience in learning their craft from their elders, be it friends or family which has passed it onto them. Like myself, most fortune-tellers have a linage which they are deeply proud and grateful of having, and that is a great dishonour to not only them but their elders who has taught the skill on them!

Each professional reader in these interviews make some good points regarding fortune-telling in the modern day.

Regarding learning personally to use a divinationary tool, I love George's method of learning and memorising the Tarot. Spending time with each suit and card in learning, and then the spiritual aspect of sleeping with it under your pillow. The mind can be a tricky thing to master such a large subject such as knowing the suits of Tarot, and associations both physically and spiritually can help greatly. Rhyming is known to be the best way to learn the cards as we see with Playing Cards as previously mentioned in this book. I wish that someday someone would do the same with tarot. I have often done similar methods myself in the past in learning a new tool of divination, such as my own method of Casting the Lots came through months of just experimenting and practicing on others, and of course mediating on the tool itself. My Scrying bowl, I learnt how to use it effectively through connecting with the Spiritworld itself, and the spirit which dwells within itself bones (or shall I say glass) of the bowl and pouring beaker.

When it comes to the actual interpretation of fortune-telling to the client, J.D makes a good point regarding to the lack of context of the query, being overly psychological & todays comfort of being overly "positive" in the reading. That much is very true in my own experience and what I have seen. In a world where science and technology seem are massively prevalent, and amongst the general population, the sense of mystery and magic is lacking in the minds of man today. Although a sense of scepticism can be quite healthy in being grounded in the physical or avoiding charlatans, the need to knit pick or take apart practices of fortune-telling can't be compared to analysing say the workings of a saw, drill, or hammer of the common trade's person. The art of divination is tangible, flexible and lays in the world of spirits and the mediator between the worlds, and often their skills are imparted onto them through natural ability to do so. As for being the tendency of being overly positive to the client for fear of anxiety or stress it may cause them but is that heathy though? Now I'm not saying telling a client when they are going to die or anything like that is helpful but how can we as readers help people improve in aspects of their lives if we can't relay as reading in areas the client is lacking or destructive in their lives. It really is the wording or way in which you relay the outcome of the reading to the client which helps to avoid anxiety or stress, and of course labelled a "bad reader".

Lisa makes a good point about the Holistic and self-help approach to divination grew in popularity during the 90's and replaced the art of prediction. As the New age movement moved forward, predictive divination was regarded as old fashioned and no longer "respectful". In the past, making predictions of future events was the heart of fortune-telling, and it was often seen as the gift of the seer or diviner, and I think its time to touch back to base and revive what fortune-telling was best known for, making predictions! Also, as Lisa mentions it was thanks to the Civil Rights movement that now people like Lisa who come from minority such as the Romani community that they protected from racism and classist views.

I hope to the reader these interviews and their conclusion has been a helpful insight in today's world of professional fortune-tellers, and the shows the hard work in which it has took for them to provide a service to their community and business. So, I shall end with a final statement:

Be Kind and respectable your fortune-teller, and do not expect more than you can deal yourself, for the world of spirits is a complicated skill to master and not many people are stronger enough to do so!

A Brief Introduction to Chapbooks

By
The National Library of Scotland

Chapbooks are small paper-covered booklets, usually printed on a single sheet or portion of a sheet, folded into books of 8, 12, 16 and 24 pages, often illustrated with crude woodcuts.

Illustration from Lumsden chapbook (1820)

They were in circulation from the 17th to the 19th centuries, sold by travelling hawkers, pedlars, street-criers or 'chapmen' for a penny or less on the streets and at markets and fairs.

The word 'chapman' is related to the word 'cheap', but it is probably also related to the Anglo-Saxon 'ceapian', meaning to barter, buy and sell.

Cheaply produced

The quality of paper used was invariably coarse. Chapbook printers frequently employed worn and broken type and it was not uncommon for the illustrations to bear no relation to the text.

Illustration from
Banbury chapbook (1800)

Chapbooks, along with broadsides, comprised the staple reading matter of the 'common people' in an age well before the arrival of harbingers of modernity such as the telegraph, the train, the telephone and the mechanised printing press.

Broad range of subjects

The subject matter of chapbooks was quite broad — sermons of covenanting ministers, prophecies, last words of murderers, songs, and poems by Robert Burns and Allan Ramsay, and biographies of famous people such as Wallace, Napoleon and Nelson. There were romances and legends, not to mention manuals of instruction and almanacs.

One of the features of this type of publication is the proliferation of provincial imprints — chapbooks were printed in places such as Fintray, Newton Stewart and Inveraray, as well as Edinburgh, Falkirk and Glasgow.

Chapbooks for children

Chapbooks were read, or perhaps more accurately, read out to people of all ages, though few publishers catered specifically for children.

James Lumsden of Glasgow was an exception — he produced good quality chapbooks for children in the early 19th century.

Reasons for decline

Chapbooks gradually disappeared from the 1860s onwards.

This was not only because of the explosion in the amount of cheap printed matter available, but also due to strong competition from religious tract societies such as the Stirling Tract Enterprise which regarded many chapbook publications as 'ungodly'.

THE
Spaewife;

OR, UNIVERSAL

FORTUNE-TELLER.

WHEREIN YOUR

FUTURE WELFARE MAY BE KNOWN,

BY

Physiognomy—Cards—Palmistry— and Coffee Grounds.

ALSO,

A DISTINCT TREATISE ON MOLES.

BY AN ASTROLOGER.

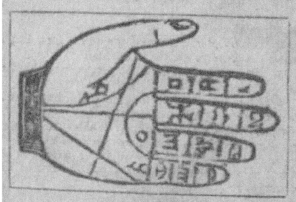

KILMARNOCK:
Printed by H. Crawford, Bookseller.
1827.

The

Spaewife;

OR, UNIVERSAL

FORTUNE-TELLER.

WHEREIN YOUR

FUTURE WELFARE MAY BE KNOWN,

BY

Physiognomy—Cards—Palmistry—and Coffee Grounds.

ALSO,

A DISTINCT TREATISE ON MOLES.

BY AN ASTROLOGER.

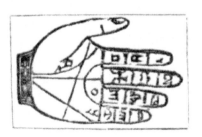

KILMARNOCK:

Printed by H. Crawford, Bookseller.

1827.

FORTUNE-TELLER.

SECRET INDICATIONS.

Judgments to be drawn from the Hair, according to the substance and colour.

THE hair is one of the most beautiful natural ornaments that adorn the head of man or woman. The Apostle Paul permits women to wear long hair as an advancement to their beauty, and to be pleasing in the eyes of their husbands.

1. Hair that is soft and thick denotes a man of much mildness.

2. When the hair hangs down and is soft, it denotes the body to decline to dryness.

3. Much hair denotes a hot person, and that he is soon angry.

4. Abundance of hair in young children shews that they increase in melancholy.

5. Curled hair and black, denotes heat; the people of the South have it most part alike.

6. Hair standing up an end, like the prickles of a hedge-hog, signifies a fearful person, and of ill courage.

Colour of the Hair.

1. White hair signifies great frigidity or cold, as may be seen in old men; but many people after much sickness, or trouble of mind, will on a sud-

FORTUNE-TELLER.

SECRET INDICATIONS.

Judgments to be drawn from the Hair, according to the substance and colour.

THE hair is one of the most beautiful natural ornaments that adorn the head of man or woman. The Apostle Paul permits women to wear long hair as an advancement to their beauty, and to be pleasing in the eyes of their husbands.

1. Hair that is soft and thick denotes a man of much mildness.

2. When the hair hangs down and is soft, it denotes the body to decline to dryness.

3. Much hair denotes a hot person, and that he is soon angry

4. Abundance of hair in young children shews that they increase in melancholy.

5. Curled hair and black, denotes heat; the people of the South have it most part alike.

6. Hair standing up an end, like the prickles of a hedge-hog, signifies a fearful person, and of ill courage.

Colour of the Hair.

White hair signifies great frigidity or cold, as may be seen in old men: but many people after much sickness, or trouble of mind, will on a sudden find their hair turn grey or white, as also after a fright or disappointment. A French Officer, aged 23, on a sudden received sentence of death; the news had such an effect on him, that before morning his hair was changed to milk white.

2. Black hair shews a person very amorous, but cruel and ungenerous.

3. Hair the colour of gold, shews a treacherous person, arbitrary and proud.

4. Dark red hair has the same signification. The perspiration of a red haired person is disagreeable.

5. Chesnut-coloured hair, or dark brown, denotes a fair, just, free, and liberal person.

The Beard.

1. A thin soft beard shews a person lustful, effeminate, of a tender body, fearful and inconstant.

2. A red beard denotes the person courteous and friendly, a great flatterer, and very soon angry.

3. A dark beard is good, yet it denotes a person to be cordial, sincere, thoughtful, and bold.

4. He that hath a decent beard, handsome, and thick of hair, is good natured and reasonable.

The Chin.

1. A long chin, denotes the person angry, and importunate in the use of words.

2. A little chin shews inveteracy and malice.

3. A round and thin chin is not manly, but womanish, and signifies boldness and much pride.

4. A square chin is manly, and denotes much courage and strength of body; and such persons are commonly given to words.

5. A round chin and dimpled shews good nature, but much addicted to pleasure.

6. A lean wrinkled chin represents a cold, impotent, and malicious person.

The Eye-brows and Eye-lids.

1. A person having much, and long hair on the eye-brows, and both join across the nose, is a very simple person, but conceited in his own opinion.

den find their hair turn grey or white, as also after a fright or disappointment. A French Officer, aged 23, on a sudden received sentence of death; the news had such an effect on him, that before morning his hair was changed to milk white.

2. Black hair shews a person very amorous, but cruel and ungenerous.

3. Hair the colour of gold, shews a treacherous person, arbitrary and proud.

4. Dark red hair has the same signification. The perspiration of a red haired person is disagreeable.

5. Chesnut-coloured hair, or dark brown, denotes a fair, just, free, and liberal person.

The Beard.

1. A thin soft beard shews a person lustful, effeminate, of a tender body, fearful and inconstant.

2. A red beard denotes the person courteous and friendly, a great flatterer, and very soon angry.

3. A dark beard is good, yet it denotes a person to be cordial, sincere, thoughtful, and bold.

4. He that hath a decent beard, handsome, and thick of hair, is good natured and reasonable.

The Chin.

1. A long chin, denotes the person angry, and importunate in the use of words.

2. A little chin shews inveteracy and malice.

3. A round and thin chin is not manly, but womanish, and signifies boldness and much pride.

4. A square chin is manly, and denotes much courage and strength of body; and such persons are commonly given to words.

5. A round chin and dimpled shews good nature, but much addicted to pleasure.

6. A lean wrinkled chin represents a cold, impotent, and malicious person.

The Eye-brows and Eye-lids.

1. A person having much, and long hair on the eye-brows, and both join across the nose, is a very simple person, but conceited in his own opinion.

2. When the eye-brows are short and narrow, denote the man good-natured and reasonable.

3. The eye-lids short and small, are thought wise and secret, yet covetous of great matters.

4. When the eye-lids are long, and long hair on the eye-lashes, they signify a person of low capacity, and false in his dealings.

The Neck.

1. He or she that hath a long neck, is of a simple nature, not secret, fearfully unlearned, a glutton, and great drinker in general.

2. He that hath a neck short and small, is wise, but deceitful, secret, constant, discreet, yet passionate and ingenious.

3. He that hath the neck fat and fleshy, is proud, wherefore he is compared to a bull, who is always ready to be angry.

4. A small neck denotes a weak understanding; if a female, she will be much inclined to sickness, and knawing of the stomach.

5. A neck inclined to the right side, denotes prudence, generosity, and curious in studies; but inclined to the left side, declares vice and impudicity.

The Eyes.

1. Great eyes denote a slothful, bold, and lying person, of a rustic and course mind.

2. Eyes deep in the head, denote a great mind, yet full of doubts, but generous and friendly.

3. Little eyes, like those of a mole or pig, denote a weak understanding, and easily imposed on.

4. Beware of squint eyes, for out of one hundred you will not find two faithful. It is very ill luck to meet a squinting person.

5. Eyes that move slowly, or look sleepy, denote an unfaithful and slothful person.

6. The worst of all the eyes are the yellowish or citron—beware of them, for the possessor is a dangerous person, if you are in his power.

7. Beware also of them, who, when they speak,

2. When the eye-brows are short and narrow, denote the man good-natured and reasonable.

3. The eye-lids short and small, are thought wise and secret, yet covetous of great matters.

4. When the eye lids are long, and long hair on the eye-lashes, they signify a person of low capacity, and false in his dealings.

The Neck.

1. He or she that hath a long neck, is of a simple nature, not secret, fearfully unlearned, a glutton, and great drinker in general.

2. He that hath a neck short and small, is wise, but deceitful, secret, constant, discreet, yet passionate and ingenious.

3. He that hath the neck fat and fleshy, is proud, wherefore he is compared to a bull, who is always ready to be angry.

4. A small neck denotes a weak understanding; if a female, she will be much inclined to sickness, and knawing of the stomach.

5. A neck inclined to the right side, denotes prudence, generosity, and curious in studies; but inclined to the left side, declares vice and impudicity.

The Eyes.

1. Great eyes denote a slothful, bold, and lying person, of a rustic and course mind.

2. Eyes deep in the head, denote a great mind, yet full of doubts, but generous and friendly.

3. Little eyes, like those of a mole or pig, denote a weak understanding, and easily imposed on.

4. Beware of squint eyes, for out of one hundred you will not find two faithful. It is very ill luck to meet a squinting person.

5. Eyes that move slowly, or look sleepy, denote an unfaithful and slothful person.

6. The worst of all the eyes are the yellowish or citron--beware of them, for the possessor is a dangerous person, if yon are in his power.

7. Beware also of them, who, when they speak,

twinkle their eyes, for they are double-minded. If it is a woman that doth so with her left eye, trust her not as to the faithfulness of her love.

But you will seldom find deceit where the eye looks with a modest confidence, not staring you out of countenance, nor averting as if detected of a crime—but when in business, love, or friendship, there appears a tender firmness.

The Nose.

1. A long nose denotes a vain mind, unruly disposition, much given to wrangling, and not to be depended on.

2. A high nose denotes a violent person, a vain liar, and extremely lascivious, easily believing another, and very inconstant.

3. He that hath a big nose every way, long and hanging down, is covetous in every thing.

4. When the nose is crooked, signifies a proud man, and him or her is never good, but justice overtakes them.

5. He that hath the nose hairy at or above the point, is a person altogether simple-hearted.

6. A Roman or acquiline nose, denotes a haughty, arbitrary, and wranglesome person.

7. A nose that is round and long, of a pleasant feature, besides being one of the perfections of beauty, denotes the woman or maid, wise, prudent, and chaste; particularly if she has blue eyes.

The Mouth.

1. He that hath a great and broad mouth is shameless, a great babbler and liar, proud to an excess, and ever abounding in quarrelsome words.

2. A little mouth denotes a person peaceable and faithful.

3. Those that have the lips small and thin, are great talkers and railers, and given to deceit and falsehood.

4. Lips that are a little thick, and well coloured, are faithful, and given to virtue; and those who

twinkle their eyes, for they are double-minded. If it is a woman that doth so with her left eye, trust her not as to the faithfulness of her love.

But you will seldom find deceit where the eye looks with a modest confidence, not staring you out of countenance, nor averting as if detected of a crime--but when in business, lore, or friendship, there appears a tender firmness.

The Nose.

1. A long nose denotes a vain mind, unruly disposition, much given to wrangling, and not to be depended on.

2. A high nose denotes a violent person, a vain liar, and extremely lascivious, easily believing another, and very inconstant.

3. He that hath a big nose every way, long and hanging down, is covetous in every thing.

4. When the nose is crooked, signifies a proud man, and him or her is never good, but justice overtakes them.

5. He that hath the nose hairy at or above the point, is a person altogether simple-hearted.

6. A Roman or acquiline nose, denotes a haughty, arbitrary, and wranglesome person.

7. A nose that is round and long, of a pleasant feature, besides being one of the perfections of beauty, denotes the woman or maid, wise, prudent, and chaste; particularly if she has blue eyes.

The Mouth.

1. He that hath a great and broad mouth is shameless, a great babbler and liar, proud to an excess, and ever abounding in quarrelsome words.

2. A little mouth denotes a person peaceable and faithful.

3. Those that have the lips small and thin, are great talkers and railers, and given to deceit and falsehood.

4. Lips that are a little thick, and well coloured, are faithful, and given to virtue; and those who

have the lips pleasantly pouting, are reckoned one of Venus's greatest beauties.

5. Those that have one lip thicker than the other, are of little understanding, slow to comprehend, and rather guilty of folly than wisdom.

The Ears.

1. Great, big, broad ears, signify a simple man, of no understanding ; sluggish, slothful, and of an ill memory.

2. Small ears denote a good understanding ; but very small ears signify nothing but mischief.

3. Those that have them long and thin, are bold, impudent, unlearned, gluttons, and whore-masters, and very proud in general.

4. Those that have them well proportioned, and neither too small nor too large, are persons of good understanding, wise, discreet, honest, shamefaced, and courageous.

The Face in general.

The face that is round, plump, and ruddy, shews the person to be of an agreeable temper, well deserving of friendship, and faithful in love.

A face with very prominent cheek bones, thin and long visage, shews a restless disposition, and rarely satisfied with any thing.

A face naturally pale, denotes the person very amorous.

Blue eyes are mostly to be depended on for fidelity, though there is never a rule without an exception, for many blue-eyed are capable of bad deeds.

Dark eyes are generally suspicious, artful, and prone to deceit.

A very fair person is in general, indifferent proud, neglectful to please, and though amorous, is too haughty to let the world believe they would think it worth the trouble of appearing agreeable.

A countenance tolerably fair, cheerful and well formed, with dark brown hair, is most to be depended on for fidelity.

have the lips pleasantly pouting, are reckoned one of Venus's greatest beauties.

5. Those that have one lip thicker than the other, are of little understanding, slow to comprehend, and rather guilty of folly than wisdom.

The Ears.

1. Great, big, broad ears, signify a simple man, of no understanding; sluggish, slothful, and of an ill memory.

2. Small ears denote a good understanding; but very small ears signify nothing but mischief.

3. Those that have them long and thin, are bold, impudent, unlearned, gluttons, and whore masters, and very proud in general.

4. Those that have them well proportioned, and neither too small nor too large, are persons of good understanding, wise, discreet, honest, shamefaced, and courageous.

The Face in general.

The face that is round, plump, and ruddy, shews the person to be of an agreeable temper, well deserving of friendship, and faithful in love.

A face with very prominent cheek bones, thin and long visage, shews a restless disposition, and rarely satisfied with any thing.

A face naturally pale, denotes the person very amorous.

Blue eyes are mostly to be depended on for fidelity, though there is never a rule without an exception, for many blue-eyed are capable of bad deeds.

Dark eyes are generally suspicious, artful, and prone to deceit.

A very fair person is in general, indifferent proud, neglectful to please, and though amorous, is too haughty to let the world believe they would think it worth the trouble of appearing agreeable.

A countenance tolerably fair, cheerful and well formed, with dark brown hair, is most to be depended on for fidelity.

MOLES.

These are little marks on the skin, although they appear to be the effect of chance or accident. and might easily pass with the unthinking for things of no moment, are nevertheless of the utmost consequence, since from their colour, situation, size, and figure, may be accurately gathered, the temper of, and the events that will happen to the person bearing them.

A Mole on the wrist, or between that and the finger ends, shews the person to be of an ingenious and industrious turn, faithful in his engagements, amorous and constant in his affections, rather of a saving disposition, with a great degree of sobriety and regularity in his dealings.

A Mole between the elbow and the wrist, shews a placid and cheerful disposition, industry, and a love of reading, particularly books of science.

A Mole near either elbow, shews a restless and unsteady disposition, with a great desire of travelling—much discontented in the marriage state, and of an idle turn.

A Mole on the right or left arm, shews a courageous disposition, great fortitude, resolution, industry, and conjugal felicity.

A Mole on the left shoulder, shews a person of a quarrelsome and unruly disposition, always inclined to dispute for trifles, rather indolent, but much inclined to the pleasures of love, and faithful to the conjugal vows.

A Mole on the right shoulder, shews a person of a prudent and discreet temper, one possessed of much wisdom, given to great secrecy, very industrious, but not very amorous, yet faithful to the conjugal ties.

A Mole on the loins, shews industry and honesty, an amorous disposition, with great vigour, courage, and fidelity.

MOLES.

These are little marks on the skin, although they appear to be the effect of chance or accident and might easily pass with the unthinking for things of no moment, are nevertheless of the utmost consequence, since from their colour, situation, size, and figure, may be accurately gathered, the temper of, and the events that will happen to the person bearing them.

A Mole on the wrist, or between that and the finger ends, shews the person to be of an ingenious and industrious turn, faithful in his engagements, amorous and constant in his affections, rather of a saving disposition, with a great degree of sobriety and regularity in his dealings.

A Mole between the elbow and the wrist, shews a placid and cheerful disposition, industry, and a love of reading, particularly books science.

A Mole near either elbow, shews a restless and unsteady disposition, with a great desire of travelling—much discontented in the marriage state, and of an idle turn.

A Mole on the right or left arm, shews a courageous disposition, great fortitude, resolution, industry, and conjugal felicity.

A Mole on the left shoulder, shews a person of a quarrelsome and unruly disposition, always inclined to dispute for trifles, rather indolent, but much inclined to the pleasures of love, and faithful to the conjugal vows.

A Mole on the right shoulder, shews a person of a prudent and discreet temper, one possessed of much wisdom, given to great secrecy, very industrious, but not very amorous, yet faithful to the conjugal ties.

A Mole on the loins, shews industry and honesty, an amorous disposition, with great vigour, courage and fidelity.

A Mole on the hip, shews that the person will have many children.

A Mole on the right thigh, shews that the person will become rich, and have good luck in marriage.

A Mole on the left thigh, denotes that the person suffers much by poverty and want of friends, as also by the enmity and injustice of others.

A Mole on the right knee, portends that the person will be rash, inconsiderate, and hasty.

A Mole on the left knee, shews a hasty and passionate disposition, with an inconsiderate turn.

A Mole on either leg, shews that the person is indolent, and indifferent as to what happens.

A Mole on either ankle, denotes a man to be inclined to effeminacy and elegance of dress; a woman to be courageous, active, and industrious.

A Mole on either foot, forbodes sudden illness, or unexpected misfortune.

A Mole that stands on the right side of the forehead or right temple, signifies that the person will arrive to sudden wealth and honour.

A Mole on the right eye brow announces speedy marriage; and that the person to whom you will be married, will possess money, amiable qualities, and a fortune.

A Mole on the outside corner of either eye, denotes the person to be of a steady, sober, and sedate disposition; but will be liable to a violent death.

A Mole on either cheek, signifies that the person never shall rise above mediocrity in point of fortune, though at the same time he will never sink to real poverty.

A Mole on both cheeks, denotes the person will know a deal of trouble, losses, and crosses, but at last arrive to be a great tradesman, and will gain great riches; will be a very public character; and also fond of rural scenes.

A Mole on the lip, either upper or lower, prevents the person to be fond of delicate things, and very

A Mole on the right hip, shews that the person will become rich, and have good luck in marriage.

A Mole on the left thigh, denotes that the person suffers much by poverty and want of friends, as also by the enmity and injustice of others

A Mole on the right knee, portends that the person will be rash, inconsiderate, and hasty.

A Mole on the left knee, shews a hasty and passionate disposition, with an inconsiderate turn.

A Mole on either leg, shews that the person is indolent, and indifferent as to what happens.

A Mole on either ankle, denotes a man to be inclined to effeminacy and elegance of dress; a woman to be courageous, active, and industrious.

A Mole on either foot, forbodes sudden illness, or unexpected misfortune.

A Mole that stands on the right side of the forehead or right temple, signifies that the person will arrive to sudden wealth and honour.

A Mole on the right eye brow announces speedy marriage; and that the person to whom you will be married, will possess money, amiable qualities, and a fortune.

A Mole on the outside corner of either eye, denotes the person to be of a steady, sober, and sedate disposition; but will be liable to a violent death.

A Mole on either cheek, signifies that the person never shall rise above mediocrity in point of fortune, though at the same time he will never sink to real poverty.

A Mole on both cheeks denotes the person will know a deal of trouble, losses, and crosses, but at last arrive to be a great tradesman, and will gain great riches; will be a very public character; and also fond of rural scenes.

A Mole on the lip, either upper or lower, prevents the person to be fond of delicate things, and very much given to the pleasures of love, in which he or she will be successful.

A Mole on the side of the neck, shews that the person will narrowly escape suffocation, but afterwards rise to great consideration by an unexpected legacy or inheritance

A Mole on the throat, denotes that the person shall become rich by marriage.

A Mole on the bosom portends mediocrity of health and fortune.

A Mole under the left breast over the heart, foreshews that man will be of a warm disposition, unsettled in mind, fond of rambling, and light in his conduct; in woman, it shews sincerity in love, quick conception, and easy to travel in child-birth.

A Mole on the belly denotes the person to be addicted to sloth and gluttony; selfish in almost all articles, and seldom inclined to be nice or careful in point of dress.

A Mole situated in those recesses which modesty conceals from view, as not to admit of being discovered but by another: and yet to have a Mole so placed is the most fortunate for them.

PALMISTRY.

THE Palms of the hands contain a great variety of lines running in different directions, every one of which bears a certain relation to the events of a person's life: and from them, with the most infallible certainty, can be told every circumstance that will happen to any one, by observing them properly. It is therefore recommended to pay a strict attention to this object, as by that means you will undoubtedly gain very excellent knowledge for your pains.

And first is given the names of the several lines as they hold their places, and then particularize their qualities.

A Mole on the hip, shews that the person will have many children.

much given to the pleasures of love, in which he or she will be successful.

A Mole on the side of the neck, shews that the person will narrowly escape suffocation, but afterwards rise to great consideration by an unexpected legacy or inheritance

A Mole on the throat, denotes that the person shall become rich by marriage.

A Mole on the bosom portends mediocrity of health and fortune.

A Mole under the left breast over the heart, foreshews that man will be of a warm disposition, unsettled in mind, fond of rambling, and light in his conduct; in woman, it shews sincerity in love, quick conception, and easy to travel in child-birth.

A Mole on the belly denotes the person to be addicted to sloth and gluttony; selfish in almost all articles, and seldom inclined to be nice or careful in point of dress.

A Mole situated in those recesses which modesty conceals from view, as not to admit of being discovered but by another; and yet to have a Mole so placed is the most fortunate for them.

PALMISTRY.

THE Palms of the hands contain a great variety of lines running in different directions, every one of which bears a certain relation to the events of a person's life: and from them with the most infallible certainty, can be told every circumstance that will happen to any one, by observing them properly. It is therefore recommended to pay a strict attention to this object, as by that means you will undoubtedly gain very excellent knowledge for your pains.

And first is given the names of the several lines as they hold their places, and then particularize their qualities.

There are five principle lines in the hand, viz:

> The Line of Life, or Life Line as it is here called.
> The Line of Death.
> The Table Line
> The Girdle of Venus.
> The Line of Fortune.

And besides these there are other Lines, as the Line of Saturn; the Liver Line, and some others, but these only serve to explain the principal Lines.

The chief Lines on which persons of the profession lay the greatest stress, is the Line of Life, or the Life Line, as it is here called, which generally takes its rise where the thumb joint plays with the wrist on the inside; and runs in an oblique direction to the inside of the innermost joint of the forefinger.

The next is the Line of Death which separates the fleshy part of the hand on the little finger side, from the hollow of the hand, running in various directions in different people.

The Table Line originates with the Life Line, at the wrist, and runs through the hollow of the hand towards the middle finger.

The Girdle of Venus takes its course from the extremity of the innermost joint of the little finger, and forming a curve, terminates between the fore and middle fingers

The Line of Fortune strikes from behind the ball, or mount of the fore finger, across the palm and Line of Life, and looses itself in or near the fleshy part of the hand on the little finger side.

If the Line of Life is crossed by other Lines at or near the wrist, the person will meet with sickness in the beginning of life, and the degree of sickness will be proportioned to the size, length, and breadth of the intervening lines. If the Life Line runs fair and uninterrupted, the person will enjoy good health; and according to its length towards the

There are five principle lines in the hand, viz.

> The Line of Life, or Life Line as it is here called.
> The Line of Death.
> The Table Line
> The Girdle of Venus.
> The Line of Fortune.

And besides these there are other Lines, as the Line of Saturn; the Liver Line, and some others, but these only serve to explain the principal Lines.

The chief Lines on which persons of the profession lay the greatest stress, is the Line of Life, or the Life Line, as it is here called, which generally takes its rise where the thumb joint plays with the wrist on the inside; and runs in an oblique direction to the inside of the innermost joint of the fore-finger.

The next is the Line of Death which separates the fleshy part of the hand on the little finger side, from the hollow on the hand, running in various directions in different people.

The Table Line originates with the Life Line, at the wrist, and runs through the hollow of the band towards the middle finger.

The Girdle of Venus takes its course from the extremity of the innermost joint of the little finger, and forming a curve, terminates between the fore and middle fingers

The Line of Fortune strikes from behind the ball, or mount of the fore finger, across the palm and Line of Life, and looses itself in or near the fleshy part of the hand on the little finger side.

If the Line of Life is crossed by other Lines at or near the wrist, the person will meet with sickness in the beginning of life, and the degree of sickness will be proportioned to the size, length, and breadth of the intervening lines. If the Life Line runs fair and uninterrupted, the person will enjoy good health; and according to its length towards outside of the fore-finger, you may judge if the person will live long, as the longer the Line the longer the Life.

If the Line of Death is short, and runs even, without being broken or divided, it shews that the person will enjoy a good length of days, and not be subject to many maladies; but if it is interrupted, it evidently shews that the person's life will be endangered by illness, but by the care of Providence will recover.

When the Table Line is broad, strong, and well marked, it shews the person to be of a sound constitution, and a peaceable contented mind: if it is broken, it shews for every break a violent interruption to happiness; if these breaks happen towards the part next the wrist, he will be crossed in love, and either be disappointed in the person he has fixed his affections on, or be saddled with a person of a disobliging temper, and a most audacious and abusive tongue.

The Girdle of Venus, when it goes on fair and well marked, shews that the person will be prosperous in love, fair in his dealings with the fair sex, and be sincerely beloved; he will obtain a partner for life of a fortune equal to his own, sweet tempered, faithful, and affectionate; but if it is interrupted at its beginning near the little finger, he will meet with early disappointments in love; if towards the middle of the line, he will ruin his health, and injure his fortune with lewd prostitutes; if near the end, he will be foolishly amorous in his old age, still expecting to gain the heart of a woman, but never will obtain it.

The Line of Fortune, by its approach to the Girdle of Venus, shews that there is a strong kindred between them, and their distance at their two extremities clearly point out that love is inconsistent with childhood, and old age; yet in those where the cross line approach from the one to the other outside of the forefinger, you may judge if the person will live long, as the longer the Line the longer the Life.

If the Line of Death is short, and runs even, without being broken or divided, it shews that the person will enjoy a good length of days, and not be subject to many maladies; but if it is interrupted, it evidently shews that the person's life will be endangered by illness, but by the care of Providence will recover.

When the Table Line is broad, strong, and well marked, it shews the person to be of a sound constitution, and a peaceable contented mind: if it is broken, it shews for every break a violent interruption to happiness if these breaks happen towards the part next the wrist, he will be crossed in love, and either be disappointed in the person he has fixed his affections on, or be saddled with a person of a disobliging temper, and a most audacious and abusive tongue.

The Girdle of Venus, when it goes on fair and well marked, shews that the person will be prosperous in love, fair in his dealings with the fair sex, and be sincerely beloved; he will obtain a partner for life of a fortune equal to his own, sweet tempered, faithful, and affectionate; but if it is interrupted at its beginning near the little finger, he will meet with early disappointments in love; if towards the middle of the line, he will ruin his health, and injure his fortune with lewd prostitutes; if rear the end, he will be foolishly amorous in his old age, still expecting to gain the heart of a woman, but never will obtain it.

The Line of Fortune, by its approach to the Girdle of Venus, shews that there is a strong kindred between them, and their distance at their two extremities clearly point out that love is inconsistent with childhood, and old age; yet in those where the cross line approach from the one to the other near the ends, prove that the persons were, or will be susceptible of love in childhood, or old age.

If the hollow palm of the hand, which some call the Plain of Mars, is full of cross lines running into each other, the person will be of a humorsome, uneven, and testy temper, jealous and hasty, quarrelsome and fighting, and endeavouring to set others by the ears; he will meet with very frequent misfortunes, and bear them very uneasily; whereas, if the hollow or palm of the hand has none but the unavoidable lines, that is to say, those that must unavoidably pass through it, he will be of a sweet and amiable disposition, full of sensibility, gratitude, and love, faithful, benevolent, and kind; and though subject to losses, crosses, and disappointments, will bear them with an even and agreeable temper; from this part chiefly, it is recommended to persons to chuse their companions for life, either for friendship or marriage.

The mount or ball of the thumb, bears a particular analogy to the events of a person's life, with respect to disputes, quarrels and lawsuits; if this mount has many long strait lines reaching from the thumb to the Line of Life, they show that the person will have several personal encounters, either with hands, clubs, pistols or swords; but if the lines are curved and crooked, they will indicate lawsuits, and according to the degree of crookedness, they will be long or short; but if these lines end in a straight direction towards the line of life, they will end prosperously, whether encounter or law suits; if otherwise, they will be attended with an unfavourable issue; the nearer to the line of life these lines begin, the later in a person's life the quarrels or law-suits will take place; and the nearer to the line of life they end, the later in life they will terminate.

near the ends, prove that the persons were, or will be susceptible of love in childhood, or old age.

If the hollow palm of the hand: which some call the Plain of Mars, is full of cross lines running into each other, the person will be of a humorsome, uneven, and testy temper, jealous and hasty, quarrelsome and fighting, and endeavouring to set others by the ears; he will meet with very frequent misfortunes, and bear them very uneasily; whereas, if the hollow or palm of the hand has none but the unavoidable lines, that is to say, those that must unavoidably pass through it, he will be of a sweet and amiable disposition, full of sensibility, gratitude, and love, faithful, benevolent, and kind; and though subject to losses, crosses, and disappointments, will bear them with an even and agreeable temper; from this part chiefly, it is recommended to persons to chuse their companions for life, either for friendship or marriage.

The mount or ball of the thumb, bears a particular analogy to the events of a person's life, with respect to disputes, quarrels and lawsuits; if this mount has many long strait lines reaching from the thumb to the Line of Life, they show that the person will have several personal encounters; either with hands, clubs, pistols or swords; but if the lines are curved and crooked, they will indicate lawsuits, and according to the degree of crookedness, they will be long or short: but if these lines end in a straight direction towards the line of life, they will end prosperously, whether encounter or lawsuits if otherwise, they will be attended with an unfavourable issue; the nearer to the line of life these lines begin, the later in a person's life the quarrels or law-suits will take place; and the nearer to the line of life they end, the later in life they will terminate

TO TELL FORTUNES BY THE GROUNDS OF A COFFEE-CUP.

Directions to pour out the Coffee-grounds.

Pour the grounds of coffee in a white cup, shake them well about in it, so that their particles may cover the surface of the whole cup; then reverse it into the saucer, that superfluous parts may be drained, and the figures required for fortune-telling be formed. The person that acts the fortune-teller must bend their thoughts upon the person that wishes their fortune told, and upon their rank and profession, in order to give plausibility to their predictions. It is not to be expected upon taking up the cup, that the figures will be accurately represented as they are in the pack, and it is quite sufficient if they bear some resemblance to any of the following emblems.

The Roads,

Or serpentine lines, indicate ways; if they are covered with clouds, they are said to be infallible marks either of past or future reverses. If they appear clear and serene, they are a sure token of some fortunate chance near at hand: encompassed with very many dots, they signify an accidental gain of money, likewise long life.

The Ring,

Signifies marriage; if a letter is near it, it denotes to the person that has his fortune told, the initial of the name of the party to be married. Likewise, if the ring is in the clear, it portends happy and lucrative friendship. Surrounded with clouds, designs that the person is to use precaution in friendship he is about to contract. If the ring appears at the bottom of the cup, it forebodes an entire separation from the beloved object.

The Leaf of Clover,

Is as well here as in common life, a lucky sign. Its different position in the cup alone makes the difference; because if it is on the top, it shews that

TO TELL FORTUNES BY THE GROUNDS OF A COFFEE CUP.

Directions to pour out the Coffee-grounds.

Pour the grounds of coffee in a white cup, shake them well about in it, so that their particles may cover the surface of the whole cup; then reverse it into the saucer, that superfluous parts may be drained, and the figures required for fortune-telling be formed. The person that acts the fortune-teller must bend their thoughts upon the person that wishes their fortune told, and upon their rank and profession, in order to give plausibility to their predictions. It is not to be expected upon taking up the cup, that the figures will be accurately represented as they are in the pack, and it is quite sufficient if they bear some resemblance to any of the following emblems.

The Roads,

Or serpentine lines, indicate ways; if they are covered with clouds, they are said to be infallible marks either of past or future reverses. If they appear clear and serene, they are a sure token of some fortunate chance near at hand: encompassed with very many dots, they signify an accidental gain of money, likewise long life.

The Ring,

Signifies marriage; if a letter is near it, it denotes to the person that has his fortune told, the initial of the name of the party to be married. Likewise, if the ring is in the clear, it portends happy and lucrative friendship. Surrounded with clouds, designs that the person is to use precaution in friendship he is about to contract. If the ring appears at he bottom of the cup, it forebodes an entire separation from the beloved object.

The Leaf of Clover,

Is as well here as in common life, a lucky sign. Its different position in the cup alone makes the difference; because if it is on the top, it shews that

78

the good fortune is not far distant; but it is subject
to delay, if it is in the middle, or at the bottom.
Should clouds surround it, it shews that many disagreeables will attend the good fortune; in the
clear, prognosticates serene and undisturbed happiness, as bright as the party wishes.

The Anchor,

The emblem of hope and commerce, implies successful business carried on by water and by land, is
on the bottom of the cup; at the top, and in the
clear part, it shews constant love, and an unshaken
fidelity. In the thick and clouded part of it also
denotes love, but tinctured with the inconstancy of
the butterfly.

The Serpent,

Always the emblem of falsehood and enmity, is
likewise here a general sign of an enemy. On the
top, or in the middle of the cup, it promises to the
consulting party the triumph which he desires over
his enemy: but he will not obtain it so easily if the
serpent be in the thick or cloudy thick. By the
letter which frequently appears near the emblem,
the enemy may easily be guessed, it makes the initial of his name.

The Letter.

By letters, we communicate to our friends either
pleasant or unpleasant news, and such is the case
here: if this emblem is in the clear part it denotes
the speedy arrival of welcome news; surrounded
with dots, it announces the arrival of a considerable
remittance in money; but hemmed in by clouds
it is quite the contrary, and forebodes some melancholy or bad tidings, a loss, or some other sinister
accident.

The Coffin,

The emblem of death, prognosticates the same
thing here, or at least a long and tedious illness,
if it be in the thick or turbid. In the clear, it denotes long life. In the thick, at the top of the cup,

the good fortune is not far distant; but it is subject to delay, if it is in the middle, or at the bottom. Should clouds surround it, it shews that many disagreeables will attend the good fortune; in the clear, prognosticates serene and undisturbed happiness, as bright as the party wishes.

The Anchor,

The emblem of hope and commerce, implies successful business carried on by water and by land, ⟨if⟩ on the bottom of the cup; at the top, and in the clear part, is shews constant love, and an unshaken fidelity. In the thick and clouded part of it also denotes love, but tinctured with the inconstancy of the butterfly.

The Serpent,

Always the emblem of falsehood and enmity, ⟨is⟩ likewise here a general sign of an enemy. On the top, or in the middle of the cup, it promises to the consulting party the triumph which he desires over his enemy: but he will not obtain it so easily if the serpent be in the thick or cloudy thick. By the letter which frequently appears near the emblem the enemy may easily be guessed, it makes the initial of his name.

The Letter.

By letters, we communicate to our friends either pleasant or unpleasant news, and such is the case here: if this emblem is in the clear part it denotes the speedy arrival of welcome news; surrounded with dots, it announces the arrival of a considerable remittance in money: but hemmed in by clouds it is quite the contrary, and forebodes some melancholy or, bad tidings, a loss, or some other sinister accident.

The Coffin,

The emblem of death, prognosticates the same thing here, or at least a long and tedious illness if it be in the thick or turbid. In the clear, it denotes long life. In the thick, at the top of the cup, it signifies a considerable estate left to the party by some rich relation; in the same manner at the bottom, it shews that the deceased is not so nearly related to the consulting party.

The Star

Denotes happiness if in the clear, and at the top of the cup; clouded, or in the thick, it signifies long life, though exposed to various vicissitudes and troubles. If dots are about it, it foretels good fortune, wealth, high respectability, &c. Several stars denote so many good and happy children; but surrounded with dashes, shews that your children will cause you grief and vexation in your old age, and that you ought to prevent it by giving them a good education in time.

The Dog,

Being at all times the emblem of fidelity or envy, has also a two-fold meaning here. At the top, in the clear, it signifies true and faithful friends; but if his image be surrounded with clouds or dashes, it shews that those whom you take for your friends are not to be depended on; but if the dog be at the bottom of the cup, you have to dread the effects of extreme envy or jealousy.

The Lily.

If this emblem be at the top, or in the middle of the cup, it signifies that the consulting party either has or will have a virtuous spouse; if it be at the bottom, it denotes quite the reverse. In the clear, the lily further betokens long and happy life; if clouded, or in the thick, it portends trouble and vexation, especially on the part of one's relation.

The Cross,

Be it one or more, it generally predicts adversities. Its position varies, and so do the circumstances. If it be at the top, and in the clear, it shews that the misfortunes of the party will soon be at an end, or that he will easily get over them; but if it appears in the middle, or at the bottom in the thick, the at the top of the cup, it signifies a considerable estate left to the party by some rich relation; in the same manner at the bottom, it shews that the deceased is not so nearly related to the consulting party.

The Star

Denotes happiness if in the clear, and at the top of the cup; clouded, or in the thick, it signifies long life, though exposed to various vicissitudes and troubles. If dots are about it, it foretels good fortune, wealth, high respectability, &c. Several stars denote so many good and happy children; but surrounded with dashes, shews that your children will cause you grief and vexation in your old age, and that you ought to prevent it by giving them a good education in time.

The Dog,

Being at all times the emblem of fidelity or envy, has also a two-fold meaning here. At the top, in the clear, it signifies true and faithful friends; but if his image be surrounded with clouds or dashes, it shews that those whom you take for your friends are not to be depended on; but if the dog be at the bottom of the cup, you have to dread the effects of extreme envy or jealousy.

The Lily.

If this emblem be at the top, or in the middle of the cup, it signifies that the consulting party either has or will have a virtuous spouse; if it be at the bottom, it denotes quite the reverse. In the clear, the lily further betokens long and happy life; if clouded, or in the thick, it portends trouble and vexation, especially on the part of one's relation.

The Cross,

Be it one or more, it generally predicts adversities. Its position varies, and so do the circumstances. If it be at the top, and in the clear, it shews that the misfortunes of the party will soon be at an end, or that he will easily get over them, but if it appears in the middle, or at the bottom in the thick, the

party must expect many severe trials: if it a
pear with dots, either in the clear or in the thic
it promises a speedy change of one's sorrow.

The Cloude.

If they be more light than dark, you may expe
a good result from your hopes; but if they a
black, you may give it up. Surrounded with do:
they imply success in trade, and in all your unde
takings; but the brighter they are, the greater wi
be your happiness.

The Sun,

An emblem of the greatest luck and happines
if in the clear; but in the thick it bodes a gre
deal of sadness; surrounded by dots or dashes d
notes that an alteration will easily take place.

The Moon.

If it appears in the clear, it denotes high honours
in the dark, or thick part, it implies sadness, whic
will, however, pass without great prejudice. Bu
if it be at the bottom of the cup, the consultin;
party will be very fortunate both by water and lan

Mountain.

If it represents only one mountain, it indicate
the favour of people of high rank, but several
them, especially in the thick, are signs of powerfu
enemies; in the clear, they signify the contrary, d
friends in high life, who are endeavouring to pro
mote the consulting party.

The Tree.

One tree only, be it in the clear or thick part
points out lasting good health; several trees denot
that your wish will be accomplished.

The Child.

In the clear part, it bespeaks innocent intercours
between the consultor and another person; in th
thick part, excesses in love matters, attended wit
great expences: at the bottom of the cup it denot
the consequences of lubidinous amours, and a ve
destructive end.

83

party must expect many severe trials: if it appear with dots, either in the clear or in the thick it promises a speedy change of one's sorrow.

The Clouds.

If they be more light than dark, you may expect a good result from your hopes; but if they are black, you may give it up. Surrounded with dots they imply success in trade, and in all your undertakings; but the brighter they are, the greater ⟨will⟩ be your happiness

The Sun,

An emblem of the greatest luck and happiness if in the clear; but in the thick it bodes a great deal of sadness; surrounded by dots or dashes denotes that an alteration will easily take place.

The Moon.

If it appears in the clear, it denotes high honours in the dark, or thick part, it implies sadness, which will, however, pass without great prejudice. But if it be at the bottom of the cup, the consulting party will be very fortunate both by water and land

Mountain.

If it represents only one mountain, it indicates the favour of people of high rank, but several ⟨of⟩ them, especially in the thick, are signs of powerful enemies; in the clear, they signify the contrary, ⟨of⟩ friends in high life, who are endeavouring to promote the consulting party.

The Tree.

One tree only, be it in the clear or thick part points out lasting good health; several trees denote that your wish will be accomplished.

The Child.

In the clear part, it bespeaks innocent intercourse between the consultor and another person; in ⟨the⟩ thick part, excesses in love matters, attended with great expences: at the bottom of the cup it denotes the consequences of lubidinous amours, and a ⟨very⟩ destructive end.

The true method of telling your Fortune, by
CARDS.

TAKE a Pack of Cards, and pick Six out of
each sort, viz. the 8, 9, 10, Knave, King & Queen,
these being the most Prophetic Cards in the Pack.
Let the Person whose Fortune is to be learned be
blindfolded. This done, let the Cards be shuffled,
and the whole dealt out singly on the table, with
their faces downwards. The bandage being then
taken off the eyes of the blinded person; he or she
must take up any one of the Cards; when, by examining the following Rules, the true Fortune may
be known. ☞ The *W.* at the beginning of each
stanza, stands for Woman, and *M.* for Man.

Eight of Diamonds.

W.—Dear miss you seem mighty uneasy,
    And look on the Cards with a frown:
The conjuror wants not to teaze ye,
    But all the bad fortune's your own.
You are doom'd for to live an old maid, ma'am,
    And never blest with your man;
But have courage, and be not afraid, ma'am,
    You'll give us the lie if you can.

The true method of telling your Fortune, by CARDS.

TAKE a Pack of Cards, and pick Six out of ⟨each⟩ sort, viz. the 8, 9, 10, Knave, King & Queen, ⟨these⟩ being the most Prophetic Cards in the Pack. ⟨Let⟩ the Person whose Fortune is to be learned be ⟨blindfolded⟩. This done, let the Cards be shuffled, ⟨and⟩ the whole dealt out singly on the table, with ⟨their⟩ faces downwards. The bandage being then ⟨taken⟩ off the eyes of the blinded person; he or she ⟨must⟩ take up any one of the Cards; when, by examining the following Rules, the true Fortune may ⟨be⟩ known. The *W.* at the beginning of each stanza, stands for Woman, and *M.* for Man.

Eight of Diamonds

⟨W⟩—Dear miss you seem mighty uneasy,
And look on the Cards with a frown:
The conjuror wants not to teaze ye,
But all the bad fortune's your own.
You are doom'd for to live an old maid, ma'am,
And never blest with your man;
But have courage, and be not afraid, ma'am,
You'll give us the lie if you can.

M.—To wander thro' your native fields,
    On rural pleasure bent ;
This Card to you that blessing yields,
    O take it as 'twas meant.
Cheerful improve each fleeting hour,
    Alas! they fly full fast ;
Do all the good within your power,
    And never dread the last.

        Nine of Diamonds.

W.—The English girl who draws this Card,
    Will have no cause to fret her ;
Yet if she thinks her fortune hard,
    She'll struggle for a better :
But if the same Card comes again,
    Old Scotland's curse attends her,
And she may scratch, and scratch again,
    Till grease and brimstone mends her.

M—Ill fate betide the wretched man,
    To whom this Card shall fall ;
His race on earth will soon be ran,
    His happiness but small.
Disloyalty shall stain his fame,
    His days be mark'd with strife,
Newgate shall record his name,
    And Tyburn end his life.

        Ten of Diamonds.

W.—Peace and plenty will attend you,
    If I happen to befriend you :
Children ten your lot will be,
    A single one, and three times three ;
But if twins you'll chance to have,
    You'll surely find an early grave.

M.—Whate'er his endeavours a man who gets this
    Shall a bachelor be all his life ;
He never shall taste of the conjugal bliss,
    Nor ever be curs'd with a wife.

        The Knave of Diamonds,

W.—Madam, your fortune's mighty queer,
    The conjuror discovers ;

M.—To wander thro your native fields,
On rural pleasure bent;
This Card to you that blessing yields,
O take it as 'twas meant.
Cheerful improve each fleeting hour,
Alas! they fly full fast;
Do all the good within your power,
And never dread the last.

Nine of Diamonds.

W.—The English girl who draws this Card,
Will have no cause to fret her;
Yet if she thinks her fortune hard,
She'll struggle for a better:
But if the same Card comes again.
Old Scotland's curse attends her.
And she may scratch, and scratch again,
Till grease and brimstone mends her.
M— Ill fate betide the wretched man,
To whom this Card shall fall;
His race on earth will soon be ran,
His happiness but small.
Disloyalty shall stain his fame,
His days be mark'd with strife,
Newgate shall record his name,
And Tyburn end his life.

Ten of Diamonds.

W.—Peace and plenty will attend you,
If I happen to befriend you:
Children ten your lot will be,
A single one, and three times three;
But if twins you'll chance to have,
You'll surely find an early grave.
M.—Whate'er his endeavours a man who gets this
Shall a bachelor be all his life;
He never shall taste of the conjugal bliss,
Nor ever be curs'd with a wife.

The Knave of Diamonds,

W.—Madam, your fortune's mighty queer,
The conjuror discovers;

To fools you'll lend a list'ning ear,
  And knaves will be your lovers.
—In Venus's wars, on London plains,
  He'll spend his early youth ;
The knave of diamonds if he gains ;
  Nay, never doubt the truth.
To prove this bold assertion just,
  Your surgeon's bill produce ;
Expose your nose, and own you must,
  That nose unfit for use.

Queen of Diamonds.
—If this queen to an amorous widow shall come,
  Who has lately interr'd a good man,
For a husband again she will quickly make
    room,
  And plague him as much as she can ;
But let her beware how she trifles with him.
  Tho' she fool'd with the sot that's departed ;
For in that case most surely her hide he will
    trim,
  Till her ladyship dies broken hearted.
—The married man that draws this card,
  Will soon a cuckold be ;
Nor let him think his fortune hard
  In so much company.
For out of twenty married pair,
  Search all the country through,
Nineteen at least the horns must wear,
  And pray why should not you.

King of Diamonds.
—Alas! poor girl, though I lament your fate,
I cannot save you from a husband's hate ;
A tyrant Lord will rule you thro' your life,
And make you curse the wretched name of wife.
—To Lords and great people frequenting the
    court,
  This card will most auspicious prove,
To the closets of princes they'll freely resort,
  And be rich in their sovereign's love.

To fools you'll lend a list'ning ear,
And knaves will be your lovers.
⟨M⟩—In Venus's wars, on London plains,
He'll spend his early youth;
The knave of diamonds if he gains;
Nay, never doubt the truth.
To prove this bold assertion just,
Your surgeon's bill produce;
Expose your nose, and own you must,
That nose unfit for use,

Queen of Diamonds.

⟨W⟩—If this queen to an amorous widow shall come,
Who has lately interr'd a good man,
For a husband again she will quickly make room,
And plague him as much as she can;
But let her beware how she trifles with him.
Tho' she fool'd with the sot that's departed;
For in that case most surely her hide he will trim,
Till her ladyship dies broken hearted.
⟨M⟩—The married man that draws this card,
Will soon a cuckold be;
Nor let him think his fortune hard
In so much company.
For out of twenty married pair,
Search all the country through,
Nineteen at least the horns must wear,
And pray why should not you.

King of Diamonds.'

⟨W⟩—Alas! poor girl, though I lament your fate,
I cannot save you from a husband's hate;
A tyrant Lord will rule you thro' your life,
And make you curse the wretched name of wife.
⟨M⟩—To Lords and great people frequenting the court,
This card will most auspicious prove.
To the closets of princes they'll freely resort
And be rich in their sovereign's love.

90

Yet in those of low rank no good it porten[d]
But oppression and hardship foreruns;
Unkind will be all their relations and frien[d]
Ungrateful their daughters and sons.

Eight of Clubs.

W.—Little peevish, crabbed elf,
Fond of no one but herself,
Cross, and still for trifles striving,
With her truly there's no living.

M.—Tho' honest you look & you speak a man fa[ir]
Yet you know you're a rascal in grain;
For sixpence your soul to the devil you'll swe[ar]
But he'll send such a thief back again.

Nine of Clubs.

W.—If this card you shall draw, O return it aga[in]
Be quick, ma'am, to take my advice;
For its only production are trouble and pain
And I hope you will not draw it twice.
But such your misfortune, I've nothing to sa[y]
To assist you is out of my power,
The stars are enacting the devil to pay,
And the play-house is open'd at four.

M—Full well I foresaw that the devil to pay,
Would harass each young female elf,
And see, my dear ladies, to help on the pla[y]
That here comes the devil himself.

Ten of Clubs.

W.—'Tis not your fortune, wit, or birth,
Can the day of death defer;
You'll soon return to parent earth,
And mix your lovely dust with her.
This will prove a mourning card.
And drown in tears the fairest face,
But her fate is no ways hard,
The lot of all the human race.

M.—Bad luck to a woman is good to man,
And it happens so often through life;
Let the man who draws this deny it if he ca[n]
For he quickly shall bury his wife.

91

Yet in those of low rank no good is ⟨portends⟩
But oppression and hardship foreruns;
Unkind will be all their relations and friends
Ungrateful their daughters and sons.

Eight of Clubs

W.—Little peevish, crabbed elf,
Fond of no one but herself,
Cross, and still for trifles striving,
With her truly there's no living.
M.—Tho' honest you look & you speak a man ⟨fair⟩
Yet you know you're a rascal in grain;
For sixpence your soul to the devil you'll swear
But he'll send such a thief back again.

Nine of Clubs.

W.—If this card you shall draw, O return it again
Be quick, ma'am, to take my advice;
For its only production are trouble and pain
And I hope you will not draw it twice.
But such your misfortune, I've nothing to say
To assist you is out of my power,
The stars are enacting the devil to pay,
And the play-house is open'd at four.
M—Full well I foresaw that the devil to pay,
Would harass each young female elf,
And see, my dear ladies, to help on the play
That here comes the devil himself.

Ten of Clubs.

W.—'Tis not your fortune, wit, or birth,
Can the day of death defer;
You'll soon return to parent earth,
And mix your lovely dust with her.
This will prove a mourning card,
And drown in tears the fairest face,
But her fate is no ways hard,
The lot of all the human race.
M.—Bad luck to a woman is good to man,
And it happens so often through life;
Let the man who draws this deny it if he can
For he quickly shall bury his wife.

Knave of Clubs.

—Though much I pity your sad fate,
Yet does my pity come too late
  To ward off fortune's rubs ;
Though you the queen of hearts should prove,
A surly brute shall gain your love,
  A very knave of clubs.
—Whatever you presume to say,
The world will talk a different way,
  Ere well your words transpire :
Ask you, good sir, the reason why,
You'll know my answer is no lie,
  No man believes a liar.

Queen of Clubs.

—Ah, Madam, too well you love kissing I find,
  My reason I scarcely need tell ye.
For while you draw this, by a fortune unkind,
  Your neighbours regard your big belly.
—And here comes the hero that got the gray
    brat,
  Lord, sir, you your blushes may spare,
For the world too well knows what you have
    been at,
  But dispel the poor lass's despair.

King of Clubs.

—This, the last, a generous card,
  Will the first of blessings prove :
Be but true, nor doubt reward,
  In a husband's faithful love.
—Of clubs the king, to you who ill portends,
Friendly yourself, you'll meet with many friends.

Eight of Hearts.

—In the days of your courtship you'll bill like a
    dove,
  But when age shall advance you'll drink hard,
Both kissing and tippling you'll show that you
    love,
  If your fortune shall send you this card.

Knave of Clubs.

⟨W⟩—Though much I pity your sad fate,
Yet does my pity come too late
To ward off fortune's rubs;
Though you the queen of hearts should prove,
A surly brute shall gain your love,
A very knave of clubs.
⟨M⟩—Whatever you presume to say,
The world will talk a different way.
Ere well your words transpire:
Ask you, good sir, the reason why,
You'll know my answer is no lie,
No man believes a liar.

Queen of Clubs.

⟨W⟩—Ah, Madam, too well you love kissing I find.
My reason I scarcely need tell ye.
For while you draw this, by a fortune unkind,
Your neighbours regard your big belly.
⟨M⟩—And here comes the hero that get the gray brat,
Lord, sir, you your blushes may spare,
For the world too well knows what you have been at,
But dispel the poor lass's despair.

King of Clubs.

⟨W⟩—This, the last, a generous card,
Will the first of blessings prove:
Be but true, nor doubt reward,
In a husband's faithful love.
⟨M⟩—Of clubs the king, to you who ill portends,
Friendly yourself, you'll meet with many friends.

———

Eight of Hearts.

⟨W⟩—In the days of your courtship you'll bill like a dove,
But when age shall advance you'll drink hard.
Both kissing and tippling you'll show that you love.
If your fortune shall send you this card.

M.—A numerous family falls to the man,
    Whose fortune shall give him this card;
So let him maintain 'em as well as he can,
    Nor grumble, or think his case hard.

Nine of Hearts.

W.—A coach and six horses will fall to the maid
    Whose first chance this card shall obtain
But if 'tis her second, I'm greatly afraid,
    She must come to plain walking again.

M.—The man however great or grand,
    Who draws the nine of hearts,
For aught that I can understand,
    Is one of shallow parts.

Ten of Hearts.

W.—Deck'd with ev'ry female grace,
    Sweet in person, mind, and face,
Thou a mother soon shall be
    With thy lovely progeny.

M.—Ten children you'll have, if this card you
    get,
    And I think you will wish for no more;
If you do try again, 'tis your fate,
    You cannot have less than a score.

Knave of Hearts.

W.—This rascally knave will your fortune con-
    found,
    Except special care you shall take;
For while scores of young lovers pour ste
    shall surround,
    You'll accept of a doting old rake.

M.—Nothing can ever save the man
    Who draws this cursed card;
A vixen will his heart trepan:
    Alas! his case is hard.

Queen of Hearts.

W.—The queen of Love will favour,
    Who draws the queen of hearts,
And many a blessing will confer;
    The fruit of female hearts.

M.—A numerous family falls to the man,
Whose fortune shall give him this card;
So let him maintain 'em as well as he can,
Nor grumble, or think his case hard.

Nine of Hearts.

W.—A coach and six horses will fall to the main
Whose first chance this card shall obtain
But if 'tis her second, I'm greatly afraid.
She must come to plain walking again.
M.—The man however great or grand,
Who draws the nine of hearts.
For aught that I can understand,
Is one of shallow parts.

Ten of Hearts.

W.—Deck'd with ev'ry female grace.
Sweet in person, mind, and face,
Then a mother soon shall be
With thy lovely progeny.
M.—Ten children you'll have, if this card you get,
And I think you will wish for no more;
If you do try again, 'tis your fate.
You cannot have less than a score.

Knave of Hearts.

W.—This rascally knave will your fortune (confound).
Except special care you shall take;
For while scores of young lovers your step; shall surround,
You'll accept of a doting old rake,
M.—Nothing can ever save the man
Who draws this cursed card;
A vixen will his heart trepan:
Alas! his case is hard.

Queen of Hearts.

W.—The queen of Love will favour,
Who draws the queen of hearts,
And many a blessing will confer;
The fruit of female hearts.

.—From girl to girl you'll often range,
 Never with one content;
But yet the oftener you shall change,
 The oftener you'll repent.

King of Hearts.

7.—If this you draw, condemn'd throughout your
  life,
 A peevish maiden, and a vixen wife;
Unchaste while married, and a widow wanton;
 All this you'll be, and more could I descant
  on.

7.—Your fortune can't be mighty good,
 For a vile whore will please you,
Who never would do what she should,
 But make your life uneasy.

Eight of Spades.

.—If youthful lasses draw the eight of spades,
 They'll toy away their time with amorous
  blades,

7.—If a doctor, lawyer, quaker, priest,
 Should fix on this card but his hand,
The conjuror swears, and he swears 'tis not,
 That some rogues will be found in the land.

Nine of Spades.

7.—The lass who gets this unlucky, hated card,
 A shrivell'd maid shall die, which you think is
  hard.

7.—How often our fortunes by opposites go;
 What brings bliss to a man, to a woman brings
  woe.

Ten of Spades.

7.—Pretty ladies, young and fair,
 Always young and debonair,
 Life with you will sweetly glide,
 And you will be a happy bride.

7.—You the happy man will prove,
 Who obtains the lady's love.

M.- From girl to girl you'll often range,
Never with one content;
But yet the oftener you shall change,
The oftener you'll repent.

King of Hearts.

W—If this you draw, condemn'd throughout your life,
A peevish maiden, and a vixen wife ;
Unchaste while married, and a widow wanton;
All this you'll be, and more could I descant on.
M—Your fortune can't be mighty good,
For a vile whore will please you,
Who never would do what she should,
But make your life uneasy,

————

Eight of Spades.

⟨*W*⟩—If youthful lasses draw the eight of spades,
They'll toy away their time with amorous blades,
⟨*M*⟩—If a doctor, lawyer, quaker, priest;
Should fix on this card but his hand,
The conjuror swears, and he swears 'tis not,
That some rogues will be found in the land.

Nine of Spades.

W—The lass who gets this unlucky, hated card,
A shrivell'd maid shall die, which you think is hard.
M—How often our fortunes by opposites go
What brings bliss to a man, to a woman brings woe

Ten of Spades.

W—Pretty ladies, young and fair,
Always young and debonair,
Life with you will sweetly glide,
And you will be a happy bride.
M—You the happy man will prove,
Who obtains the lady's love.

Knave of Spades.

W.—If this knave you should obtain,
 Put him in the pack again;
  For the rascal brings all kinds of news,
  Such as you must never chuse.

M.—Of all the cards throughout the pack,
 No worse to man can come;
  His wife will stun him with her clack,
  And make him hate his home.

Queen of Spades.

W.—An elegant behaviour makes the lass,
 Through whose fair hand this card shall pass

M.—The rule of contrarieties we see,
 Of man, the most unhappy he,
  Who this ill-fated card shall take,
  His wife will be a perfect rake.

King of Spades,

W.—The ladies of fashion this card who obtain,
 In vain on the court may attend,
  His Majesty's favours they never will gain,
  Nor find at St. James's a friend.

M.—But a contrary fate on the man will attend,
 His king will some favours bestow;
  The poor and the wretched he'll often befriend
  And cherish the children of woe.

FINIS.

Knave of Spades.

W.—If this knave you should obtain,
Put him in the pack again;
For the rascal brings all kinds of news,
Such as you must never chuse.
M.—Of all the cards throughout the pack,
No worse to man can come;
His wife will stun him with her clack,
And make him hate his home.

Queen of Spades.

W.—An elegant behaviour makes the lass,
Through whose fair hand this card shall pass
M.—The rule of contrarieties we see,
Of man, the most unhappy he,
Who this ill-fated card shall take,
His wife will be a perfect rake.

King of Spades.

W.—The ladies of fashion this card who obtain,
In vain on court may attend
His Majesty's favours they never will gain,
Nor find at St. James's a friend.
M.—But a contrary fate on the man will attend,
His king will some favours bestow;
The poor and the wretched he'll often befriend
And cherish the children of woe.

FINIS.

Editions of The Spaewife Chapbook

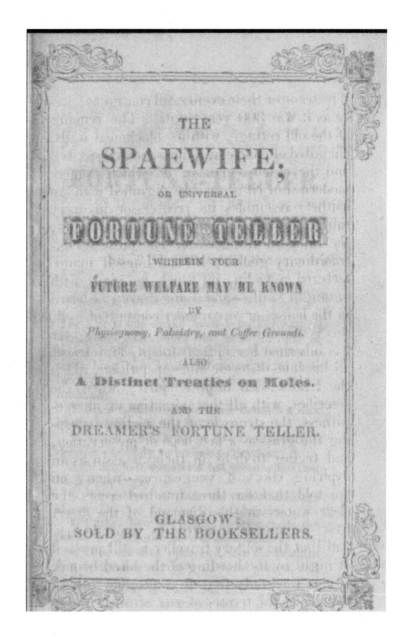

THE
SPAEWIFE,

OR UNIVERSAL

FORTUNE TELLER

WHEREIN YOUR

FUTURE WELFARE MAY BE KNOWN

BY

Physiognomy, Palmistry, and Coffee Grounds.

ALSO

A Distinct Treatise on Moles.

AND THE

DREAMER'S FORTUNE TELLER.

GLASGOW,
SOLD BY THE BOOKSELLERS.

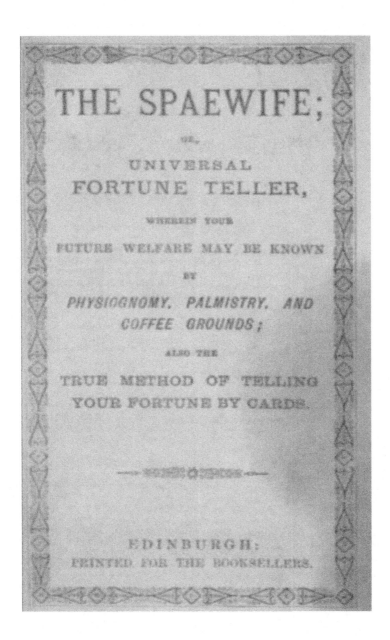

THE SPAEWIFE;

OR,

UNIVERSAL
FORTUNE TELLER,

WHEREIN YOUR

FUTURE WELFARE MAY BE KNOWN

BY

PHYSIOGNOMY, PALMISTRY, AND
COFFEE GROUNDS;

ALSO THE

TRUE METHOD OF TELLING
YOUR FORTUNE BY CARDS.

EDINBURGH:
PRINTED FOR THE BOOKSELLERS.

THE
Spaewife:

OR, UNIVERSAL

FORTUNE-TELLER.

WHEREIN YOUR

FUTURE WELFARE MAY BE KNOWN,

BY

*Physiognomy—Cards—Palmistry—
and Coffee Grounds.*

ALSO,

A DISTINCT TREATISE ON MOLES.

BY AN ASTROLOGER.

FALKIRK:

PRINTED FOR THE BOOKSELLERS.

THE
SPAEWIFE;
OR UNIVERSAL
FORTUNE-TELLER,

WHEREIN YOUR

FUTURE WELFARE MAY BE KNOWN,

BY

Physiognomy, Cards, Palmistry, and Coffee Grounds.

ALSO,

A Distinct Treatise on Moles.

PRINTED FOR THE BOOKSELLERS.

THE TRUE

FORTUNE TELLER;

OR

UNIVERSAL BOOK OF FATE.

Containing besides other valuable information, directions by which any one may know under what planet he was born.—An account of the evil and perilous days of every month of the year.—How to choose a husband or wife by the hair, eyes, &c., &c.

GLASGOW:
PRINTED FOR THE BOOKSELLERS.

The True

FORTUNE TELLER;

OR

UNIVERSIAL BOOK OF FATE

*Containing besides other valuable information, directions by which any
One may know under what planet he was born,--An account of the evil,
And perilous days of every month of the year.—How to choose a husband
Or wife by the hair, eyes, etc, etc.*

EXPLANATION OF THE TREE OF FATE

OBSERVE.-That you may either pick a number blind folded amidst the leaves of this valuable tree, or throw for them with dice ; if you pick for them and get among the branches, or in the blank leaves, it shows a speedy misfortune or disappointment at hand. The mark number of 1000 shows a great advancement in life, if you are so fortunate as to hit on it.

1 Gifts of Money
2 Prosperous run of business
3 Speedy Marriage
4 Many Children
5 A good partner in marriage
6 You will become rich
7 Money through love
8 Cash by Trade
9 A rise in Life
10 A long journey
11 Anger and discontent
12 An important journey
13 A letter that will alter your present circumstances
14 Mind what you say to a lover
15 Present from a distance
16 Dispute with one you love
17 A lawsuit
18 Visit from a distant friend
19 Party of pleasure
20 Preferment
21 Love at first sight
22 A prize worth having
23 Wealth and dignity.

24 Visit to a foreign land
25 Profit by industry
26 Prosperity by marriage
27 A multitude of cares
28 By friends you will profit
29 Second partner better than first
30 Surmount many difficulties
31 A false friend
32 A pleasing surprise
33 A change in your affairs
34 A ramble by moonlight
35 Scandal
36 Unpleasing tidings
37 Loss in a short time
38 A christening
39 Get rich through a legacy
40 Change your situation
41 New wearing apparel
42 A speedy present
43 News from sea
44 Pleasant paths in future
45 You will be asked a question of importance to-morrow

TO THE

READER

In ushering into the world such a performance as this, it may be necessary to give our readers some account of the life of the person who left the following little work for the benefit and instruction of the world, a person whose fame, though not recorded among the roll of those whose heroic actions have trumpeted them to the world, yet her discerning eye, and her knowledge in prescience, render her not unknown to the generality of those who devote any attention to this interesting study.

Mrs Bridget, vulgarly called Mother Bridget, lived, in her peregrinage through this life, in a kind of cave, or rather a hollow, formed by nature above ground, with the assistance of a little art, and comprising an exceeding warm shelter from the air: company of all sorts resorted to her, nobility, gentry, tradesmen, and mechanics—men, women, girls, and boys, of all degrees and classes.

Our heroine was born on the spot where she lived, and from the most juvenile part of her life betokened an early propensity to prescience, which

TO THE

READER

———

In ushering into the world such a performance as this, it may be necessary to give our readers some account of the life of the person who left the following little work for the benefit and instruction of the world, a person whose fame, though not recorded among the roll of those whose heroic actions have trumpeted them to the world, yet her discerning eye, and her knowledge in prescience, render her not unknown to the generality of those who devote any attention to this interesting study.

Mrs Bridget, vulgarly called Mother Bridget, lived, in her peregrinage through this life, in a kind of cave, or rather a hollow, formed by nature above ground, with the assistance of a little art, and comprising an exceeding warm shelter from the air: company of all sorts resorted to her, nobility, gentry, tradesmen, and mechanics-men, women, girls, and boys, of all degrees and classes.

Our heroine was born on the spot where she lived, and from the most juvenile part of her life betokened an early propensity to prescience, which evinced she had it instincted in her by nature. Her parents dying when she was young, left her to ramble abroad at her will; and she supported herself chiefly by begging. It was then strongly remarked in her, that she made observations on people's features and manners; would sit up whole nights when the atmosphere was clear, and seemed as intent on considering the stars, as the greatest astrologers would be with their glasses; this gave her a great knowledge of the weather, the alteration of the air, and the effect it had; and from her sometimes casually acquainting the neighbouring farmers of any change which generally took place, her fame began to spread when young, and she was consulted by them on almost every occasion; not a farmer would go to plough, not a sower would put the seed in the ground, without first asking the young gipsey (for so they then styled her) her opinion, and following according to her dictates.

Her fame now began to spread, and Bridget's prescience became more universal; other persons besides farmers and her neighbours came to consult her, and the truth of her predictions made her veracity gain ground, and she became the topic of conversation of the politest circles, many of whom came in their equipages to consult her; and she never asked for any particular sum, so the unbounded generosity of those who applied to her oracles, put her in possession of more money than was sufficient to maintain her.

As she grew in years, like the generality of old

evinced she had it instincted in her by nature. Her parents dying when she was young, left her to ramble abroad at her will; and she supported herself chiefly by begging. It was then strongly remarked in her, that she made observations on people's features and mannors; would sit up whole nights when the atmosphero was clear, and seemed as intent on considering the stars, as the greatest astrologers would be with their glasses; this gave her a great knowledge of tho weather, the alteration of the air, and the effect it had; and from her sometimes casually acquainting the neighbouring farmers of any change which generally took place, her fame began to spread when young, and she was consulted by them on almost every occasion; not a farmer would go to plough, not a sower would put the seed in the ground, without first asking the young gipsey (for so they then styled her) her opinion, and following according to her dictates.

Her fame now began to spread, and Bridget's prescience became more universal; other persons besides farmers and her neighbours came to consult her, and the truth of her perdictions made her veracity gain ground, and she became the topic of conversation of the politest circles, many of whom came in their equipages to consult her; and she never asked for any particular sum, so the unbounded generosity of those who applied to her oracles, put her in possession of more money than was sufficient to maintain her.

As she grew in years, like the generality of old

folks, she became fond of dumb animals, which were her chief companions; and of those she always had numbers; people, indeed, have said hundreds, and others have declared she could call as many on the earth as she pleased; but this is fabulous, for I never saw more than ten at a time. Dogs and cats were the principal companions of her retirement, which, being of the smallest breed, would, as she sat, creep from different parts of her garments, and not a little surprise those that came to see her, and, indeed, frightened many; though, to do her justice, she desired her visitors not to be terrified at her domestics, as she termed them, for they were not like many that attended on the gentry, saucy, imperious, and unfaithful, but were always attendant on the will of her whose hand fed them, nor would injure without provocation, a lesson, she used to say, she wished was learned by all mankind.

Of a pipe of tobacco our Bridget was exceedingly fond, and, indeed, was continually whiffing; and as she indeed, humourously used to observe, she had "sent more puffs into the world, than all the quacks in the kingdom;" from a long contracted habit, likewise, when she was smoking, of ever being seated so that her knees almost touched her visage, her limbs became so contracted, that when she became in years, she was almost double, which, together with her enormous length of nose and chin, her pipe, and the number of animals about her, made her cut a most hideous figure, and appear rather uncommonly terrifying to those who were not apprised of it.

folks, she became fond of dumb animals, which were her chief companions; and of these she always had numbers; people, indeed, have said hundreds, and others have declared she could call as many en the earth as sho pleased; but this is fabulous, for I never saw more than ten at a time. Dogs and cats were the principal companions of her retirement, which, being of the smallest breed, would, as she sat, creep from different parts of her garments, and not a little surpriso those that came to see her, and, indeed, frightened many; though, to do her justice, she desired her visitors not to be terrified at her domestics, as she termed them, for they were not like many that attended on the gentry, saucy, imperieus, and unfaithful, but were always attendant on the will of her whose hand fed them, nor would injure without provocation, a lesson, she used to say, she wished was learned by all mankind.

Of a pipe of tobacco our Bridget was cxceedingly fond, and, indeed, was continually whiffing; and as she indeed, humourously used to observe, she had "sent more puffs into the world, than all the quacks in the kingdom;" from a long contracted habit, likewise, when sho was smoking, of ever being seated so that her knees almost touched her visage, her limbs became so contracted, that when she became in years, sho was almost double, which, together with her enormous length of nose and chin, her pipe and the number of animals about her, made her cut a most hideous figure, and appear rather uncommonly terrifying to those who were not apprised of it.

6

Though this famous old woman had never been taught to write, yet by long practice she had formed to herself a kind of hieroglyphical characters, in which she decyphered her observations, knowledge, and remarks; these I found concealed within the thatch of her cave; but as they were so unintelligible, I thought it would be impossible to make head or tale of such a heap of monsters, and other figures as were attempted to be drawn; but as I am rather of a studious turn, I thought as I had made it my business formerly to transcribe the Egyptian hieroglyphics, which, when they were as unintelligible to me as these, I might by perseverance get at the depth of this valuable manuscript, or at least it would serve to deposit in the British Museum, as the remains of a woman who was so famous, and whose name was so well known among mankind.

I was therefore immediately determined on renewing my labours with redoubled ardour and unwearied application; and at length, as perseverance and resolution will conquer difficulties, I found it, and the whole mystery was opened unto me. Think of my joy: not the miser who has found a treasure he supposed lost; not a maiden who finds her lover returned after a long voyage, whom she thought perished in the waves, but finds restored to her arms with love and fidelity; not—but a truce with metaphors—it is enough to tell the reader that I was at length enabled to read this valuable work, and found by experience, that the maxims and remarks, her observations and judgement, have been

Though this famous old woman had never been taught to write, yet by long practice she had formed to herself a kind of hieroglyphical characters, in which she decyphered her observations, knowledge, and remarks; those I found concealed within the thatch of her cave: but as they were so unintelligible, I thought it would be impossible to mako head or tale of such a heap of monsters, and other figures as were attempted to be drawn; but as I am rather of a studious turn, I thought as I had made it my business formerly to transcribe the Egyptian hieroglyphics, which, when they were as unintelligible to me as these, I might by perseverance get at the depth of this valuable manuscript, or at least it would serve to deposit in the British Museum, as the remains of a woman who was so famous, and whose name was so well known among mankind.

I was therefore immediately determined on renewing my labours with redoubled ardour and unwearied application; and at length, as perseverance and resolution will conquer difficulties, I found it, and the whole mystery was opened unto me. Think of my joy: not the miser who has found a treasure he supposed lost; not a maiden who finds her lover returned after a long voyage, whom she thought perished in the waves, but finds restored to her arms with love and fidelity; not—but a truce with metaphors—it is enough to tell the reader that I was at length enabled to read this valuable work, and found by experience, that the maxims and remarks, her observations and judgement, have been extensive, are true, strongly characteristic, and would do honour to the most experienced astrologers.

Nature sometimes in her roughest coat drops her brightest jewel, which for a long time lies hid till developed by some experienced adept. So we may observe of our authoress, that though clothed in the meanest garb, nature showed herself in her abilities, and left it for me to hand down to posterity what otherwise would be lost in oblivion.

Thinking, therefore, so precious a jewel should not remain long hid, but shed its lustre to all eyes, I immediately set about putting it into English; which at length I have accomplished, and usher it into the world, requesting the gentle reader to excuse my literal errors; and if he reaps any benefit from this production, I shall not think my labour ill bestowed, though all the merit is due to the deceased authoress.

extensive, are true, strongly characteristic, and would do honour to the most experiencod astrologers.

Naturo sometimes in her roughest coat drops her brightest jewel, which for a long time lies hid till developed by somo experienced adept. So we may observe of our authoress, that though clothed in the meanest garb, nature showed herself in her abilities, and left it for me to land down to posterity what otherwise would be lost in oblivion.

Thinking, therefore, so precious a jewel should not remain long hid, but shed its lustre to all eyes, I immediately set about putting it into English; which at length I have accomplished, and usher it into the world, requesting the gentlo reader to excuse my literal errors; and if he reaps any benefit from this production, I shall not think my labour all bestowed, though all the merit is due to the deceased authoress.

THE TRUE

FORTUNE TELLER.

---

*An Explanation of the Circles of the Sphere, and
some other Terms of Astrology, for the easier Understanding of this Book, and further information
of the Reader.*

The Equinoctial circle, Equator, or Equinox, is
a great circle or line, equally distant from the two
poles of the world, dividing the sphere in the
midst.

Zodiac is a broad oblique circle, crossing the
equinoctial in two opposite places, viz., in the beginning of Aries and that of Libra, so that one
half declines towards the south ; and in this circle
is comprehended the twelve constellations or signs,
every sign containing thirty degrees in length, and
twelve in breadth. Note also, that the first six are
northern signs, and the last six southern signs.

The Ecliptic line, is a line imagined to go along
in the midst of the Zodiac as a girdle, out of which
the sun never goes ; but the moon and other planets
are sometimes on the one side, and sometimes on
the other side, which is called their latitudes, only
the fixed stars alter not their latitudes, whether
great or small ; but the longtitude of a star is the
arch, or parts of the ecliptic in degrees, between the
beginning of Aries, and the circle which passeth
through the body of the stars ; where note, that

FORTUNE TELLER

———

An Explanation of the Circles of the Sphere, and some other Terms of Astrology, for the easier Understanding of this Book, and further information of the Reader.

The Equinoctial circle, Equator, or Equinox, is a great circlo or line, oqually distant from the two poles of the world, dividing the sphere in the midst.

Zodiac is a broad oblique circle, crossing the equinoctial in two opposite places, viz., in the boginning of Aries and that of Libra, so that one half declines towards the south; and in this circle is comprehended the twelve constellations or signs, every sign containing thirty degrees in length, and twelve in breadth. Noto also, that the first six are northern signs, and tho last six southern signs.

The Ecliptic lino, is a line imagined to go along in tho midst of the Zodiac as a girdle, out of which the sun never goes; but the moon and othcr planets are sometimes on the one side, and sometimes on tho other side, which is callcd thcir latitudcs, only the fixed stars alter not their latitudes, whether great or small; but the longtitude of a star is the arch, or parts of the ecliptic in degrees, betweon the beginning of Aries, and the circle which passeth through tho body of the stars; where note, that all the circles of the sphere, or heavens, whether they are large or small, have 360 degrees allowed to each of them.

Colours are said to be two great moveable circles, crossing each other at the poles of the world, one cutting the equinox at the beginning of Aries, Cancer, and Capricorn, and so dividing the globe into four equal parts.

Horizon is a great circle which divideth the upper hemisphere, that is, the upper part of the world, from the lower, we always being supposed to be between.

Meridian is a great circle passing through the pole of the world, and the poles of the horizon, called the Zenith and Nadir, (which are two points, one directly over our heads, the other directly under our feet) on which the sun is always just at noon, and to go directly north and south, the meridian is changed; but to go to east and west, it is changed to sixty miles, either way makes one degree, or four minutes of time difference under the equinox, viz. 60 miles eastward, it is noon four minutes sooner, and sixty miles westward, four minutes later.

Tropics are supposed to be two lesser circles, parallel with the equinoctial, and distant from it on either side 23 degrees 31 minutes each; the ecliptic line touches the tropics of Cancer on the north side of the equinoctial, and it touches the tropics of Capricorn on the south side thereof, so that the sun hath his motion between these two circles.

The Arctic circle is equally distant from the north pole, as the tropics are distant from the equinox—23 degrees 31 minutes.

The Antarctic circle is the same distance from the south pole.

Zones, so called, are five in number, two cold, two temperate, and one hot, which are divided by all tho circles of the sphere, or heavens, whether they aro large or small, have 360 degrees allowed to each of them.

Colours are said to be two great moveable circles, crossing each other at tho poles of the world, one cutting the equinox at the beginning of Aries, Cancer, and Capricorn, and so dividing the globo into four equal parts.

Horizon is a great circle which divideth the upper hemisphere, that is, the upper part of the world, from the lower, we always being supposed to bo between.

Moridian is a great circlo passing through the polo of tho world, and the poles of the horizon, called the Zenith and Nadir, (which are two points, ono directly over our heads, the other directly under our feet) on which tho sun is always just at noon, and to go directly north and south, the meridian is changed; but to go to east and west, it is changed to sixty miles, either way makes one degree, or four minutes of time difference under the equinox, viz. 60 miles eastward, it is noon four minutes sooner, and sixty miles westward, four minutes later.

Tropics aro supposed to be two lesser circles, parallol with the equinoctial, and distant from it on either sido 23 degrees 31 minutes each; tho eclipic lino touches the tropics of Cancer on tho north sido of the equinoctial, and it touches tho tropics of Capricorn on the south side thereof, so that the sun hath his motion botween these two circles.

The Arctic circle is equally distant from tho north pole, as the tropics are distant from tho equinox-23 degrees 31 minutes.

The Antarctic circle is the same distance from the south pole.

Zones, so called, are five in number, two cold, two temperate, and one hot, which are divided by the tropics and polar circles from each other; the hot zone is counted between the two tropics that are extended from one to the other, being about 47 degrees 2 minutes broad; the temperate zones are extended from the tropics, on either side, to about 42 degrees 58 minutes, that is northward to the article circle, and southward to the antarctic circle and the two cold zones are each within those two small circles, having the poles for their centre.

The Poles of the world—two points exactly opposite to each other in the heavens, one in the north, the other in the south, the earth being in the midst, so that it seems to turn about as if it were borne up by them; therefore by some it is termed the axle-tree of the world, as if there was a line supposed to be drawn from one pole through the centre of the earth to the other, and the earth turning thereon; though Holy Writ tells us— "The Lord hangeth the earth upon nothing, it being upheld by his mighty power." The pole arctic, or north pole. is elevated above our horizon about 51 degrees, and the stars within that distance from it never set with us, but keep their course round it daily; so likewise those that are that distance from the south pole never rise with us, but perform their course in the like order.

Azimuths are supposed lines, or circles of distance from the meridian, drawn from the zenith to any degree, or two degrees of the horizon, or according to the 32 points of the mariner's compass, so that in travelling or sailing any way, supposing a circle to go from our zenith directly before us to the horizon, is the azimuth. called the vertical point, as well as the zenith.

Almicantharats, or Almadarats, or circles of Altitude, are imagined lines passing through the meridian parallel with the horizon.

The Sphere is a round body representing the

the tropics and polar circles from each other; the hot zone is counted between the two tropics that are extended from one to the other, being about 47 degrees 2 minutes broad; the temperate zoues are extended from the tropics, on either side, to about 42 degrees 58 minutes, that is northward to the article circle, and southward to the antarctic circle and the two cold zones are each within those two small circles, having the poles for their centre.

The Poles of the world-two points exactly opposite to each other in the heavens, one in the north, the other in the south, the earth being in the midst, so that it seems to turn about as if it were borne up by them; therefore by some it is termed the axle-tree of the world, as if there was a line supposed to be drawn from one pole through the centre of the earth to the other, and the earth turning thereon: though Holy Writ tells us-"The Lord hangeth the earth upon nothing, it being upheld by his mighty power." The pole arctic, or north pole, is elevated above our horizon about 51 degrees, and the stars within that distance from it never set with us, but keep their course round it daily; so likewise those that are that distance from the south pole never rise with us, but perform their course in the like order.

Azimuths are supposed lines, or circles of distance from the meridian, drawn from the zenith to any degree, or two degrees of the horizon, or according to the 32 points of the mariner's compass, so that in travelling or sailing any way, supposing a circle to go from our zenith directly before us to the horizon, is the azimuth, called the vertical point, as well as the zenith.

Almicantharats, or Almadarats, or circles of Altitude, are imagined lines passing through the meridian parallel with the horizon.

The Sphere is a round body representing the

frame of the whole world, as the circle of the heaven and the earth. This is sometimes called a martial sphere, for the orbs of the planets are called their spheres, that is, the circles in which they move.

Ascension is the rising of any star, or any part of the ecliptic above the horizon—Descension is its going down.

Right ascension of a star, is that part of the equinox that riseth or setteth with a star in the right sphere; but an oblique sphere, is that part of the equinoctial in degrees, containing between the first point of Aries, and that part of the equinoctial which passeth by the meridian with the centre of the star.

Oblique ascenison is a part of the equinoctial in degrees containing between the beginning of Aries and that of the equinox, which rises with any star or part of the ecliptic in an oblique sphere.

Essential difference is the difference between the right and oblique ascension, or the number of degrees contained between that place and the equinox that riseth with the centre of a star, and that place of the equinox that cometh to the meridian with the same star.

Solstice is in the summer when the sun is in the beginning of Cancer; and in the winter when the sun enters into Capricorn: because then the days seem to stand still, and seem neither to increase or decrease above two minutes in ten or twelve days.

Constellation is a certain number of stars supposed to be limited within some form or likeness; as Aries the Ram is said to have thirteen stars;—Taurus the Bull, thirty-three; Arcturus, Orion, and the Pleiades, mentioned in Job, ix. 9, are said to be constellations.

Planets are the seven erratique, or wandering stars, called Saturn, Jupiter, Mars, Venus, Mercury, frame of the whole world, as the circle of the heaven and the earth. This is sometimes called a martial sphere, for the orbs of the planets are called their spheres, that is, the circles in which they move.

Ascension is the rising of any star, or any part of the ecliptic above the horizon-Descension is its going down.

Right ascension of a star, is that part of the equinox that riseth or setteth with a star in the right sphere; but an oblique sphere, is that part of the equinoctial in degrees, containing between the first point of Aries, and that part of the equinoctial which passeth by the meridian with the centre of the star.

Oblique ascenison is a part of the equinoctial in degrees containing between the beginning of Aries and that of the equinox, which rises with any star or part of the ecliptic in an oblique sphere.

Essential difference is the difference between the right and oblique ascension, or the number of degrees contained between that place and the equinox that riseth with the centre of a star, and that place of tho equinox that cometh to the meridian with the same star.

Solstice is in the summer when the sun is in the beginning of Cancer: and in the winter when the sun enters into Capricorn: because then the days seem to stand still, and seem neither to increaso or decrease above two minutes in ten or twelve days.

Constellation is a certain number of stars supposed to be limited within some form or likeness; as Aries the Ram is said to have thirteen stars;-Taurus the Bull, thirty-three: Arcturus, Orion, and the Pleiades, mentioned in Job, ix. 9, are said to be constellatiads.

Planets are the seven cratique, or wandering stars, called Saturn, Jupiter, Mars, Venus, Mercury,

12

Sol, and Luna. These planets have also their several motions, as—

Direct, is a planet moving in its natural course, which is forward.

Retrograde, is their moving backward, contrary to their direct motion.

Combust is their being under the sun's beams, or within eight degrees of it.

Oriental, is when a planet riseth before the sun, —Occidental, after him.

Latitude of the earth is the distance or breadth on either side of the equinox towards the pole, and they that are under the equinox have no latitude, but the poles of the world are in the horizon. This is a right sphere, and every 60 minutes directly north and south, are said to make a degree of latitude in an oblique sphere; as London is counted to be in 51 degrees 32 minutes, the pole thereof being exalted as much. The like is to be observed in any other place or region.

Longitude of the earth is the outside thereof, extending from west to east, crossing the latitude at right angles; the beginning of which (according to some astronomers) is the Canary Isles, so going eastward quite round the world, unto the same place again, which is 360 degrees: and under the equinoctial is reputed to be 29,600 miles, reckoning 60 miles to a degree; but tho farther off the equinoctial the fewer miles in a degree; for at London about 37 make a degree of longitude, so these degrees grow less and less, until they meet at the latitude of 90, that is under the poles.

Parallels—the lines straight and circular, equally distant from each other, as the equinox, tropics, degrees of latitude, &c.

Climate, or clime, is such a space of earth comprehended between two parallels, in which space there is half an hour difference in the sun dials and length of the days.

Sol, and Luna. These planets have also their several motions, as-

Direct, is a planet moving in its natural course, which is forward.

Retrograde, is their moving backward, contrary to their direct motion.

Combust is their being under the sun's beams, or within eight degrees of it.

Oriental, is when a planet riseth before the sun,-Occidental, after him.

Latitude of the earth is the distance or breadth on either side of the equinox towards the pole, and they that are under the equinox have no latitude, but the poles of the world are in the horizon. This is a right sphere, and every 60 minutes directly north and south, are said to make a degree of latitude in an oblique sphere; as London is counted to be in 51 degrees 32 minutes, the pole thereof being exalted as much. The like is to be observed in any other place or region.

Longitude of the earth is the outside thereof, extending from west to east, erossing the latitude at right angles; the beginning of whieh (aceording to some astronomers) is the Canary Isles, so going eastward quite round the world, nnto the same place again, which is 360 degrees: and under the equinoctial is reputed to be 29,600 miles, reekoning 60 miles to a degree; but tho farther off the equinoctial the fewer miles in a degreo; for at London about 37 make a degree of longitude, so these degrees grow less and less, until they meet at the latitude of 90, that is under the poles.

Parallels - the lines straight and eircular, equally distant from each other, as the equinox, tropics, degrees of latitude, &c.

Climate, or clime, is such a space of earth comprehended between two parallels, in which space there is half an hour difference in the sun dials and length of the days.

13

Antipodes are those whose feet are directly against ours; as if a line were drawn from one through the centre of the earth to the other.

And this shall suffice for an explanation of things, which I have done as briefly as I could for the advantage of the reader; to whom possibly, these things so necessary to be known, may have hitherto been concealed.

Of the Planetary Days and Hours, and how to know what Planet a Man is born under.

The planetary hours are those hours in which each planet reigns, and has the chief dominion: of which the ancients gave the following account.

Saturn is lord on Saturday—Jupiter lord on Thursday—Mars is lord on Tuesday—Sol is lord on Sunday—Mercury on Wednesday—Venus on Friday—and Luna on Monday.

On Saturday, the first hour after midnight, Saturn reigns, the second Jupiter, the third Mars, the fourth Sol, the fifth Venus, the sixth Mercury, and the seventh Luna; and then again Saturn the eight, and so on to Mars the 24th; and then Sol beginneth the first hour after midnight on Sunday, Venus the 2d, and so on; Luna the first on Monday, and Saturn the 2d; Mars the first on Tuesday, Sol the 2d, and so forward, planet by planet, according to their order, by which every planet reigns the first hour of his own day; and so likewise the eighth, fifteenth, and twenty-second; as for instance Saturn reigns the first hour, the eighth, fifteenth, and twenty-second, on Saturday, Sol the same hours on Sunday, Luna the same on Monday, Mars the same on Tuesday, Mercury the same on Wednesday, Jupiter the same on Thursday, and so Venus on Friday, which I have thus set.

Antipodes are those whose feet are directly against ours; as if a line were drawn from one through the centre of the earth to the other.

And this shall suffice for an explanation of things, which I have done as briefly as I could for the advantage of the reader; to whom possibly, these things so necessary to be known, may have hitherto been concealed.

Of the Planetary Days and Hours, and how to know what Planet a Man is born under.

The planetary hours are those hours in which each planet reigns, and has the chief dominion: of which the ancients gave the following account.

Saturn is lord on Saturday-Jupiter lord on Thursday-Mars is lord on Tuesday-Sol is lord on Sunday—Mercury on Wednesday-Venus on Friday-and Luna on Monday.

On Saturday, the first hour after midnight, Saturn reigns, the second Jupiter, the third Mars, the fourth Sol, the fifth Venus, the sixth Mercury, and the seventh Luna; and then again Saturn the eight, and so on to Mars the 24th; and then Sol beginneth the first hour after midnight on Sunday, Venus the 2d, and so on; Luna the first on Monday, and Saturn the 2d; Mars the first on Tuesday, Sol the 2d, and so forward, planet by planet, according to their order, by which every planet reigns the first hour of his own day; and so likewise the eighth, fifteenth, and twenty-second; as for instance Saturn reigns the first hour, the eighth, fifteenth, and twenty-second, on Saturday, Sol the same hours on Sunday, Luna the same on Monday, Mars the same on Tuesday, Mercury the same on Wednesday, Jupiter the same on Thursday, and so Venus on Friday, which I have thus set.

	Sunday	Monday	Tuesday	Wednesday	Thursday	Friday	Saturday
Saturn	5 12 19	2 9 16 23	6 13 20	3 10 17 24	7 14 21	4 11 18	1 8 15 22
Jupiter	6 13 20	3 10 17 24	7 14 21	4 11 18	1 8 15 22	5 12 19	2 9 16 23
Mars	7 14 21	4 11 18	1 8 15 22	5 12 19	2 9 16	6 13 20	3 10 17 24
Sol	1 8 15 22	5 12 19	2 9 16 23	6 13 20	3 10 17 24	7 14 21	4 11 18
Venus	2 9 16 23	6 13 20	3 10 17 24	7 14 21	4 11 18	1 8 15 22	5 12 19
Mercury	3 10 17 24	7 14 21	4 11 18	1 8 15 22	5 12 19	2 9 16 23	6 13 20
Luna	4 11 18	1 8 15 22	5 12 19	2 9 16 23	6 13 20	3 10 17 24	7 14 21

This is so easy it needs little explanation; its use is to find what planet rules any hour of the day and every day in the week. As for example—I desire to know what planet rules on Wednesday, at 8 o'clock at night; under Wednesday I look for 20, which answers to 8 o'clock at night; for the natural day, consisting of 24 hours begins at midnight, so that from 12 at noon you begin to reckon 13, 14, 15, 16, &c. you find that the 20th hour from midnight answers to 8 o'clock at night, over against which, on the left hand, you find Sol, which shows that to be the hour of the sun. And if you would know what planet rules at 7 in the morning of that day, you will find it against 7, which shows you that Venus rules that hour; and so of any hour in the day.

		Monday	Tuesday	Wednesday	Thursday	Friday	Saturday
Saturn	Sunday	2 9 16 23	6 13 20	3 10 17 24	7 14 21	4 11 18	1 8 15 22
Jupiter	5 12 19	3 10 17 24	7 14 21	4 11 18	1 8 15 22	5 12 19	2 9 16 23
Mars	6 13 20	4 11 48	1 8 15 22	5 12 19	2 9 16	6 13 20	3 10 17 24
Sol	7 14 21	5 12 79	2 9 16 23	6 13 20	3 10 17 24	7 14 21	4 11 18
Venus	1 8 15 22	6 13 20	3 10 17 24	7 14 21	4 11 18	1 8 15 22	5 12 19
Mercury	2 19 16 23	7 14 21	4 11 18	1 8 15 22	5 12 19	2 9 16 23	6 13 20
Luna		1 18 15 22	5 12 19	2 9 16 23	6 13 20	3 10 17 24	7 14 21

This is so easy it needs little explanation; its use is to find what planet rules any hour of the day and every day in the week. As for example-I desire to know what planet rules on Wednesday, at 8 o'clock at night: under Wednesday I look for 20, which answers to 8 o'clock at night; for the natural day, consisting of 24 hours begins at midnight, so that from 12 at noon you begin to reckon 13, 14, 15, 16, &c. you find that the 20th hour from midnight answers to 8 o'clock at night, over against which, on the left hand, you find Sol, which shows that to be the hour of the sun. And if you would know what planet rules at 7 in the morning of that day, you will find it against 7, which shows you that Venus rules that hour ; and so of any hour in the day.

15

But I shall now come to speak of the significa-tion of the planetary hour of each planet, and what it portends to them that are born in them.

The hour of Saturn is strong, is good to do all things that require strength ; such as fighting, bear-ing burdens, and the like ; but for those things it is very evil. He that is born in the hour of Saturn is slow, dull, and melancholy, of dogged temper and disposition, black and swarthy complexion, being quarrelsome, wrathful, and very malicious.

The hour of Jupiter is in all things good, and denotes peace, love, and concord. He that is born in the hour of Jupiter is of a ruddy and sandy com-plexion, fair hair, well-proportioned body, and of a lovely countenance ; his face rather broad than long. He is also courteous, of a very affable car-riage, moral, and religious.

The hour of Mars is evil, and denotes the per-son born in it to be of a choleric disposition, and of a robust strong body, soon angry, and hard to be reconciled ; his face red, and his eyes sparkling and fiery, much addicted to fighting, and ready to quarrel with every man he meets, which often brings him to an untimely end.

The hour of the Sun signifies great strength, very fortunate for kings and princes. He that is born in this hour has sharp eyes, brown hair, and a round face, denotes one that is a great projector, aims at great things, but is often disappointed, and seldom brings his design to pass.

The hour of Venus is very propitious and for-tunate, but it is better by night than by day, es-pecially mid-day, for the sun covers it. He that is born in this hour has fair hair, soft eyes, a little forehead, and a round beard, very complaisant in his carriage, mighty amorous, a great admirer of women, much addicted to singing and gaming, and spends his money in courting and treating the fair sex.

But I shall now come to speak of the signification of the planetary hour of each planet, and what it portends to them that are born in them.

The hour of Saturn is strong, is good to do all things that require strength; such as fighting, bearing burdens, and the like; but for those things it is very evil. He that is born in the hour of Saturn is slow, dull, and melancholy, of dogged temper and disposition, black and swarthy complexion, being quarrelsome, wrathful, and very malicious.

The hour of Jupiter is in all things good, and denotes peace, love, and concord. He that is born in the hour of Jupiter is of a ruddy and sandy complexion, fair hair, well-proportioned body, and of a lovely countenance; his face rather broad than long. He is also courteous, of a very affable carriage, moral, and religious.

The hour of Mars is evil, and denotes the person born in it to be of a choleric disposition, and of a robust strong body, soon angry, and hard to be reconciled; his face red, and his eyes sparkling and fiery, much addicted to fighting, and ready to quarrel with every man he meets, which often brings him to an untimely end.

The hour of the Sun signifies great strength, very fortunate for kings and princes. He that is born in this hour has sharp eyes, brown hair, and a round face, denotes one that is a great projector, aims at great things, but is often disappointed, and seldom brings his design to pass.

The hour of Venus is very propitious and fortunate, but it is better by night than by day, especially mid-day, for the sun covers it. He that is born in this hour has fair hair, soft eyes, a little forehead, and a round beard, very complaisant in his carriage, mighty amorous, a great admirer of women, much addicted to singing and gaming, and spends his money in courting and treating the fair sex.

16

The hour of Mercury is very good, but chiefly from the beginning to the middle. He that is born in this hour, has stature inclining to tallness, a sharp long face, large eyes, a long nose, his forehead narrow, a long beard, and thin hair, long arm and fingers, of a good disposition, and obliging temper, much given to reading, and very desirous of knowledge, delighting to be among books, very eloquent in his speech, and yet addicted to lying, and if he is poor, he is commonly light fingered.

The hour of the moon is both good and evil, according to the day: for from the fourth to the seventeenth it is good to those that are born under it; but from the seventeenth to the twentieth it is counted unfortunate to be born under it; and from the twentieth to the twenty-seventh very happy. He that is born in the hour of the moon (especially upon her own day) shall be pale faced, of a thin meagre visage, with hollow eyes, and of a middling stature; he appears very courteous and obliging, but is very crafty and deceitful, variable in his humour, malicious, and his constitution phlegmatic.

Thus have I given the reader the judgment of ancients upon the planetary hours, and what they portend to those that are born under them, by which a person, comparing himself to what is here set down, may easily know under what planet he was born.

Of the Birth of Children with respect to the Age of the Moon.

To be born the first day of the new moon, is very fortunate, for to such all things shall succeed well; their sleep will be sweet, and their dreams pleasant; they shall have long life and increase of riches.

The hour of Mercury is very good, but chiefly from the beginning to the middle. He that is born in this hour, has stature inclining to tallness, a sharp long face, large eyes, a long nose, his forehead narrow, a long beard, and thin hair. long arms and fingers, of a good disposition, and obliging temper, much given to reading, and very desirous of knowledge, delighting to be among books, very eloquent in his speech, and yet addicted to lying, and if he is poor, he is commonly light fingered.

The hour of the moon is both good and evil, according to the day: for from the fourth to the seventeenth it is good to those that are born under it; but from the seventeenth to the twentieth it is counted unfortunate to be born under it; and from the twentieth to the twenty-seventh very happy. He that is born in the hour of the moon (especially upon her own day) shall be pale faced, of a thin meagre visage, with hollow eyes, and of a middling stature; he appears very courteous and obliging, but is very crafty and deceitful, variable in his humour, malicious, and his constitution phlegmatic.

Thus have I given the reader the judgment of ancients upon the planetary hours, and what they portend to those that are born under them, by which a person, comparing himself to what is here set down, may easily know under what planet he was born.

Of the Birth of Children with respect to the Age of the Moon.

To be born tho first day of the new moon, is very fortunate, for to such all things shall succeed well; their sleep will be sweet, and their dreams pleasant: they shall have long life and increase of riches.

17

A child born the second day of the new moon shall grow apace ; but it will be much inclined to lust, whether it be male or female. On this day also, all thy dreams shall quickly come to pass, whether they be good or bad. It is also good on this day to open a vein if there be occasion.

A child born on the third day of the moon shall die soon, or at least short-lived ; on this day to begin any work of moment is unfortunate, for it seldom comes to a good conclusion.

On the fourth day of the moon the child that is born shall prosper in the world, and be of good repute. On this day it is good to begin any enterprise, provided it be done with good advice, and with dependence on Heaven for a blessing.

The fifth day of the moon is unfortunate : and the child that is born therein shall die in its infancy. He that is in danger, and thinks to escape this day shall certainly be mistaken. If good counsel be given thee to-day take it, but execute it to-morrow. This day thou may let blood with good success.

The sixth day of the moon the child that is born shall be of long life, but very sickly. To send children to school on this day is very fortunate, and denotes they shall increase in learning.

On the seventh day the child that is born may live many years; on this day it is good to shave the head, to tame wild beasts, and buy hogs, for he that doth so shall gain much by them, he that takes physic this day is like to recover.

On the eighth day a child born shall be in danger of dying young ; but if he survives his first sickness, he shall live long and arrive at a great estate. He that dreams a dream shall quickly have it come to pass. Any thing that is lost shall be found.

On the ninth day the child that shall be born shall be very fortunate, enjoying long life, and arriving to great riches. What thou undertakest this

A child born the second day of the new moon shall grow apace; but it will be much inclined to lust, whether it be male or female. On this day also, all thy dreams shall quickly como to pass, whether they be good or bad. It is also good on this day to open a vein if there be occasion.

A child born on the third day of the moon shall die soon, or at least short-lived; on this day to begin any work of moment is unfortunate, for it seldom comes to a good conclusion.

On the fourth day of the moon the child that is born shall prosper in the world, and be of good repute. On this day it is good to begin any enterprise, provided it be done with good advice, and with dependence on Heaven for a blessing.

The fifth day of the moon is unfortunate; and the child that is born therein shall die in its infancy. He that is in danger, and thinks to escape this day shall certainly be mistaken. If good counsel be given thee to-day take it, but execute it to-morrow. This day thou may let blood with good success.

The sixth day of the moon the child that is born shall be of long life, but very sickly. To send children to school on this day is very fortunate, and denotes they shall increaso in learning.

On the seventh day the child that is born may livo many years; on this day it is good to shave the head, to tame wild beasts, and buy hogs, for he that doth so shall gain much by them, he that takes physic this day is like to recover.

On the eighth day a child born shall be in danger of dying young; but if he survives his first sickness, he shall live long and arrive at a great estate. He that dreams a dream shall quickly have it come to pass. Any thing that is lost shall be found.

On the ninth day the child that shall be born shall be very fortunate, enjoying long life, and arriving to great riches. What thou undertakest this day shall come to a good issue; he that is pursued shall escape; and he that groans under the burden of oppression, shall be opportunely relieved. Do not let blood on this day, for it is dangerous.

On the tenth day a child that is born shall be a great traveller, pass through many kingdoms and regions, and at last die at home in his old age. Do nothing on this day but what you would have known, for all secrets shall be brought to light

On the eleventh day of the moon the child that is born shall be of a good constitution, and be mightily devoted to religion, shall be long-lived, and of a lovely countenance; and if it be a female, she shall be endowed with wisdom and learning. On this day it is good to marry, for the married couple shall be happy all their lives, and be blessed with many children.

The twelfth day of the moon's age, in allusion to the twelfth sign of the Zodiac, betokeneth nothing but sorrow and woe: and the child born this day shall be given to wrathfulness, and subject to many afflictions.

On the thirteenth day the child that is born shall be of a short life, and by reason of peevish crossness never be pleased. To wed a wife on this day is good, for she shall be both loving and obedient to her husband.

On the fourteenth day the child that is born shall be an enemy to his country, and seek the destruction of his prince, which shall bring him to his deserved end. On this day if you give to a sick man physic, it shall restore him to his former health.

On the fifteenth day the child that is born shall quickly die. On this day begin to work for it is fortunate. That which was lost yesterday will be found this day.

On the sixteenth day the child born shall be of ill manners, and very unfortunate, insomuch that day shall come to a good issue; he that is pursued shall escape; and he that groans under tho burden of oppression, shall be opportunely relieved. Do not lot blood on this day, for it is dangerous.

On the tenth day a child that is born shall be a great traveller, pass through many kingdoms and regions, and at last die at home in his old age. Do nothing on this day but what you would have known, for all secrets shall be brought to light

On the eleventh day of the moon the child that is born shall be of a good constitution, and be mightily devoted to religion, shall bo long-lived, and of a lovely countenance; and if it be a female, sho shall be endowed with wisdom and learning. On this day it is good to marry, for the married couple shall bo happy all their lives, and be blessed with many children.

The twelfth day of the moon's age, in allusion to the twelfth sign of the Zodiac, betokeneth nothing but sorrow and woe: and the child born this day shall be given to wrathfulness, and subject to many afflictions.

On the thirteenth day the child that is born shall be of a short life, and by reason of peevish crossness never be pleased. To wed a wife on this day is good, for she shall be both loving and obedient to hor husband.

On the fourteenth day the child that is born shall be an enemy to his country, and seek the destruction of his prince, which shall bring him to his deserved end. On this day if you give to a sick man physic, it shall restore him to his former health.

On the fifteenth day the child that is born shall quickly die. On this day begin to work for it is fortunate. That which was lost yesterday will be found this day.

On the sixteenth day the child born shall be of ill manners, and very unfortunate, insomuch that though he may live long, yet his life will be a burden to him. It is not good to dream on this day for they are commonly hurtful, and such as come to pass a long time after.

On the seventeenth day the child that shall be born will be foolish to that degree, that it shall be almost a natural, and thereby become a great affliction to its parents; yet to contract matrimony, compound physical preparations, and take physic is very good; but by no means let blood.

On the eighteenth day the child that shall be born, if male, will be violent, courageous, and eloquent; and if female, chaste, industrious, and beautiful, and shall come to honour in her old age.

On the nineteenth day the child then born, if a male, shall be renowned for wisdom and virtue, and thereby arrive to great honour: but if a female, she will be of a weak and sickly constitution, yet she will live to be married.

On the twentieth day the child that shall be born shall be stubborn, quarrelsome, and a great fighter, yet he shall arrive to riches and a great store of money.

On the one and twentieth day the child that is born will be unhappy, and though he will be witty and ingenious, yet he shall be addicted to stealing. He that is minded to keep his money, ought on this day to abstain from gaming, else he may chance to lose all. Abstain from bleeding this day.

On the twenty-second day the child born shall be fortunate and purchase a good estate; he shall also be of a cheerful countenance, comely, and religious, and shall be well loved.

On the three and twentieth day the child born shall be of an ungovernable temper, and will give himself up to wandering abroad in the world, and seeking his fortune in foreign parts, and in the end though he may live long, yet his life will be a burden to him. It is not good to dream on this day for they are commonly hurtful, and such as come to pass a long time after.

Ou the seventeenth day the child that shall be born will be foolish to that degree, that it shall be almost a natural, and thereby become a great affliction to its parents; yet to contract matrimony, compound physical preparations, and take physic is very good; but by no means let blood.

Ou the eighteenth day the child that shall be born, if male, will be violeut, courageous, and eloquent; and if female, chaste, industrious, and beautiful, and shall come to honour in her old age.

On the nineteenth day the child then born, if a male, shall be renowned for wisdom and virtue, and thereby arrive to great honour: but if a female, she will be of a weak and sickly constitution, yet she will live to be married.

On the twentieth day the child that shall be born shall be stubborn, quarrelsome, and a great fighter, yet he shall arrive to riches and a great store of money.

On the one and twentieth day the child that is born will be unhappy, and though he will be witty and ingenious, yet he shall be addicted to stealing. He that is minded to keep his money, ought on this day to abstain from gaming. else he may chance to lose all. Abstain from bleeding this day.

On the twenty-second day the child born shall be fortunate and purchase a good estate; he shall also be of a cheerful countenance, comely, and religious, and shall be well loved.

On the three and twentieth day the child born shall be of an ungovernable temper, and will give himself up to wandering abroad in the world, and seeking his fortune in foreign parts, and in the end shall be mistaken. This is a good day to wed a wife; for ho that can meet with a good wife ought to marry her while he can have her.

On the Twenty-fourth day the child then born shall be a prodigy in the world, and make all men admire his surprising wonderful actions, which shall exceed those of the ordinary sort of men.

On the five and twentieth day the child then born shall bo wicked, he shall encounter with many dangers and at last will perish by them. This is an unfortunate day to those who begin any enterprize of moment thereon.

On the six and twentieth day the child that shall bo then born shall be very beautiful and amiable; but yet of an indifferent state in the world, if it be a male; but if it be a female, a rich man marries her for her beauty.

The twenty-seventh day the child that shall bo born shall be of that sweet and affable temper and disposition, that it will contract tho love of every one with whom it shall converse: and yet if a male shall never rise to any great height in the world: but if a maiden, the sweetness of her disposition may advance her, for such a temper is to be esteemed above riches.

On the twenty-eighth day the child that is born shall be the delight of his parents, but yet subject to much sickness and many distempers, which shall take it away before it is at perfect age.

On the twenty-ninth day the child that shall be born shall be fortunate and happy, blessed with long life, and attain to an eminent degree of holiness, wisdom, and virtue. To marry a good wife is a good fortune, and such shall be his that shall marry on this day.

On the thirtieth day the child that shall be born will be fortunate and happy, and well skilled in arts and sciences shall be mistaken. This is a good day to wed a wife; for ho that can meet with a good wife ought to marry her while he can have her.

On the Twenty-fourth day the child then born shall be a prodigy in the world, and make all men admire his surprising wonderful actions, which shall exceed those of the ordinary sort of men.

On the five and twentieth day the child then born shall bo wicked, he shall encounter with many dangers and at last will perish by them. This is an unfortunate day to those who begin any enterprize of moment thereon.

On the six and twentieth day the child that shall bo then born shall be very beautiful and amiable; but yet of an indifferent state in the world, if it be a male; but if it be a female, a rich man marries her for her beauty.

The twenty-seventh day the child that shall be born shall of that sweet and affable temper and disposition, that it will contract tho love of every one with whom it shall converse: and yet if a male shall never rise to any great height in the world: but if a maiden, the sweetness of her disposition may advance her, for such a temper is to be esteemed above riches.

On the twenty-eighth day the child that is born shall be the delight of his parents, but yet subject to much sickness and many distempers, which shall take it away before it is at perfect age.

On the twenty-ninth day the child that shall be born shall be fortunate and happy, blessed with long life, and attain to an eminent degree of holiness, wisdom, and virtue. To marry a good wife is a good fortune, and such shall be his that shall marry on this day.

On the thirtieth day the child that shall be born will be fortunate and happy, and well skilled in arts and sciences

These, and divers other like things, happen to mankind according to the different ages and courses of the moon, which has a great influence upon all human bodies.

I will, therefore, for the advantage and benefit of my readers, treat a little more distinctly of the powers and influences of the heavenly bodies, as they are laid down by ancient and modern astrologers, who have written upon that subject more largely.

A brief Prognostication concerning Children born on any day of the Week.

The child born on Sunday shall be of a long life and obtain riches.

On Monday. Weak and of an effeminate temper, which seldom brings a man to honour.

On Tuesday. Worse, though he may with extraordinary violence, conquer the inordinate desires to which he will be subject, still he will be in danger of dying by violence, if he has not great precaution.

On Wednesday. Shall be given to the study of learning, and shall profit thereby.

On Thursday. He shall arrive at great honour and dignity.

On Friday. He shall be of a strong constitution, and perhaps lecherous.

On Saturday. This is another bad day, nevertheless the child may come to good, though it be but seldom ; but most children born on this day are of a heavy, dull, and dogged disposition.

Of the evil and perilous Days of every Month of the Year.

There are certain days in the year which it concerns all persons to know, because they are so pe-

These, and divers other like things, happen to mankind according to the different ages and courses of the moon, which has a great influence upon all human bodies.

I will, therefore, for the advantage and benefit of my readers, treat a little more distinctly of the powers and influences of the heavenly bodies, as they are laid down by ancient and modern astrologers, who have written upon that subject more largely.

A brief Prognostication concerning Children born on any day of the Week.

The child born on Sunday shall be of a long life and obtain riches.

On Monday. Weak and of an effeminate temper, which seldom brings a man to honour.

On Tuesday. Worse, though he may with extraordinary violence, conquer the inordinate desires to which he will be subject, still he will be in danger of dying by violence, if he has not great precaution.

On Wednesday. Shall be given to the study of learning, and shall profit thereby.

On Thursday. He shall arrive at great honour and dignity.

On Friday. He shall be of a strong constitution, and perhaps lecherous.

On Saturday. This is another bad day, nevertheless the child may come to good, though it be but seldom; but most children born on this day are of a heavy, dull, and dogged disposition.

Of the evil and perilous Days of every Month of the Year.

There are certain days in the year which it concerns all persons to know, because they are so rilous and dangerous ; for on these days if a man or woman let blood, they shall die within twenty-one days following ; and whosoever falleth sick on any of these days shall certainly die ; and whosoever beginneth any journey on any of these days he shall be in danger of death before he returns. Also he that marrieth a wife on any of these days they shall either be quickly parted, or else live together with sorrow and discontent. And lastly, whosoever on any of these days beginneth any great business, it will never prosper or come to the desired perfection.

Now, since these days are so unfortunate, it highly concerns every one, both to know and take notice of them ; which that the reader may do, I have set down in the following order :—

In January are eight days, that is to say, the 1st, 2d, 4th, 5th, 10th, 15th, 17th, and 19th.

In February are three days, that is, the 8th, 17th and 21st.

In March are three days, that is, the 13th, 16th, and 21st.

In April are two, the 15th and 21st.

In May three, the 15th, 17th, and 20th

In June two, the 4th, and 5th.

July two, the 15th, and 20th.

In August two, the 10th, and 25th.

In September two, the 6th, and 7th.

In October one, the 19th.

In November two, the 5th and 7th.

In December three, the 6th, 7th, and 11th.

But besides these, there are also the canicular, or dog days, which are those of the greatest danger and peril ; they begin the 19th day of July, and end the 27th of August, during which time it is very dangerous to fall sick, take physic, or to let blood ; but if necessity call for it, it is best to be done before the middle of the day.

perilous and dangerous; for on these days if a man or woman let blood, they shall die within twenty-ono days following; and whosoever falleth sick on any of these days shall certainly die; and whosoever beginneth any journey on any of these days he shall be in danger of death before he returns. Also he that marrieth a wife on any of these days they shall either he quickly parted, or else live together with sorrow and discontent. And lastly, whosoever on any of these days beginneth any great business, it will never prosper or come to the desired perfection.

Now, since these days are so unfortunate, it highly concerns every one, both to know and take notice of them : which that the reader may do, I have set down in the following order:---

In January are eight days. that is to say, the 1st, 2d, 4th, 5th, 10th, 15th, 17th, and 19th.

In February are three days, that is, the 8th, 17th and 21st.

In March are three days, that is, the 13th, 16th, and 21st.

In April are two, the 15th and 21st.

In May three, the 15th, 17th, and 20th

In June two, the 4th, and 5th.

July two, the 15th, and 20th.

In August two, the 10th, and 25th.

In September two, the 6th, and 7th.

In October one, the 19th.

In November two, the 5th and 7th.

In December three, the 6th, 7th, and 11th.

But besides these, there are also the canicular, or dog days, which are those of the greatest danger and peril; they begin the 19th day of July, and end the 27th of August, during which time it is very dangerous to fall sick, take physic, or to let blood; but if necessity call for it, it is best to be done before the middle of the day.

JUDGMENTS DEDUCED FROM THE NAILS.

They who have their nails broad, are of a gentle disposition, bashful, and afraid of speaking before their superiors, or indeed to any without hesitation and a downcast eye.

If round the nails there is usually any excoriation, or sprouting of the skin, the person is luxurious, fearful, and an epicure, loving enjoyment, provided it is to be obtained without danger.

When there are certain white marks at the end, it testifies that the person is improvident, soon ruining their fortune through negligence.

Narrow Nails. The person with such nails is desirous of attaining knowledge in the sciences : but is never at peace long with his neighbours.

When to narrowness they add some degree of length, the person is led away by ambitious desires, aiming at things he cannot obtain ; one who, having formed notions of grandeur, grasps at the shadow while he loses the substance.

If at both ends there is a redness, or mixture of several colours, the person is choleric, and delights in fighting.

When the end is black, the man loves agriculture ; he places happiness in mediocrity, and from thence avoids the cares attendant on either extreme of fortune.

Round nails declare a hasty person, yet good-natured, and very forgiving, a lover of knowledge, honest in mind, doing no one any harm, and acting according to his own imagination, being rather too proud of his own abilities.

Long Nails. When the nails are long the person is good-natured, but placing confidence in no man, being from his youth conversant in deceit,

JUDGMENTS DEDUCED FROM THE

NAILS.

They who have their nails broad, are of a gentle ⟨disposition⟩, bashful, and afraid of speaking before ⟨their⟩ superiors, or indeed to any without hesitation ⟨and⟩ a downcast eye.

If round the nails there is usually any excoriation, or sprouting of the skin, the person is luxurious, fearful, and an epicure, loving, enjoyment, ⟨provided⟩ it is to be obtained without danger.

When there are certain white marks at the end, ⟨it⟩ testifies that the person is improvident, soon mining their fortune through negligence.

Narrow Nails. The person with such nails is ⟨desirous⟩ of attaining knowledge in the sciences: ⟨but⟩ is never at peace long with his neighbours.

When to narrowness they add some degree of ⟨length⟩, the person is led away by ambitious desires, ⟨aiming⟩ at things he cannot obtain; one who, having formed notions of grandeur, grasps at the ⟨shadow⟩ while he loses the substance.

If at both ends there is a redness, or mixture of ⟨several⟩ colours, the person is choleric, and delights ⟨in⟩ fighting.

When the end is black, the man loves agriculture; he places happiness in mediocrity, and ⟨from⟩ thence avoids the cares attendant on either ⟨extreme⟩ of fortune.

Round nails declare a hasty person, yet good-natured, and very forgiving, a lover of knowledge, ⟨honest⟩ in mind, doing no one any harm, and acting according to his own imagiuation, being rather ⟨too⟩ proud of his own abilities.

Long Nails. When the nails are long the person is good-natured, but placing confidence in no ⟨man⟩, being from his youth conversant in deceit, yet not practising it, from the goodness of his nature and a love of virtue.

Fleshy Nails. A calm person and idler, lov— to sleep, eat, and drink; not delighting in busk and a busy life.

Little Nails. Little round nails discover a pe son to be obstinate, seldom pleased, inclining to hate every one, as conceiving himself superior to others though without any foundation for such conception.

Pale or Lead-coloured Nails. A melancholy person, one who through choice leads a sedentary life, and would willingly give up all things for the sake of study.

Red and Spotted Nails. Choleric and martial delighting in cruelty and war; his chief pleasure being in plundering of towns, where every feroci ous particle in human nature is glutted to satiety.

When upon the nails you find any black spots they always signify evil, as white ones are a toke of good.

White Nails. When the nails are white un long, the person is subject to great sickness; he well-made and comely, but much inclined women, who deceive him through false pretence and shortly bring him to ruin.

If upon the white there appear pale lead-coloure spots, a short life and addicted to melancholy.

TO THE READER.

yet not practising it, from the goodness of his nature and a love of virtue.

Fleshy Nails. A calm person and idler, low to sleep, eat, and drink; not delighting in buck aud a busy life.

Little Nails. Little round nails discover a person to be obstinate, seldom pleased, inclining to hate every one, as conceiving himself superior to others, though without any foundation for such conception

Pale or Lead-coloured Nails. A melancholy person, one who through choice leads a sedentary life, and would willingly give up all things for ⟨the⟩ sake of study.

Red and Spotted Nails. Choleric and martial, delighting in cruelty and war; his chief ⟨pleasure⟩ being in plundering of towns, where every ferocious particle in human nature is glutted to satiety.

When upon the nails you find any black spots, they always signify evil, as white ones are a ⟨token⟩ of good.

White Nails. When the nails are white ⟨and⟩ long, the person is subject to great sickness; he ⟨is⟩ well-mado and comely, but much inclined ⟨to⟩ women, who deceive him through false pretences and shortly bring him to ruin.

If upon the white there appear pale lead-coloured spots, a short life and addicted to melancholy.

TO THE READER.

The foregoing pages are published principally to show the superstitions which engrossed the mind of the population of ⟨Scotland⟩ during a past age, and which are happily disappearing before ⟨the⟩ progress of an enlightened civilization. It is hoped, ⟨therefore⟩ that the reader will not attach the slightest importance to ⟨the⟩ solutions of the dreams as rendered above, as dreams are ⟨generally⟩ the result of a disordered stomach, or an excited imagination.

Propitious and Unpropitious days to undertake a project or event.

The Propitious days, *Bodleian MS lat. Litug, e. 10, circa 1440:*

Theys venderwrytyn to þe perilous dayes for to take eny sekenes in, or to be huete in, or to be weddyd in, or to take eny journey vpon, or to begynne eny werke in þat he wold wele spedde. The noumbre of theys dayes be in the yere xxxij. Þat be theys:

(These are understood to be the perilous days for taking any skills in, or to be on this day in, or to be wedded in, or to take any journey upon, or to begin any work in what he would well spend. The number of these days be the year 1440, that be these)

In Janivere (January) beth iij, the j, þe iijth, þe v, the vij, the x and the xv. [1st, 2nd, 4th, 5th,7th, 10th, 15th]

In Feverere (February) beth iij: the vj, þe vij & the xviij [6th, 7th, 18th]

In March beth iij: the j, þe vj, the viij [1st, 6th, 8th]

In Aprill beth ij: the vj & the the x [6th, 11th]

In May beth iij: þe v, þe vi & þe vij [5th, 6th, 7th]

In June beth ij: þe vij & þe xv. [5th, 15th]

In July beth ij: þe v & the xix. [5th, 19th]

In August beth ij: þe xv & þe vij. [15th, 9th]

In septembre beth ij: þe vj and þe vij. [6th, 7th]

In Octotre beth j: the vi. [2nd, 6th]

In Nouembre beth ij: the xv & þe xvi. [15th, 16]

In Decembre beth iij: þe xvi þe xvj & þe xvij. [16th, 16th?, 17th]

Sedt amen In domino Confido. (But still I trust in the Lord)

Chapter 4: Divination Part I, *The Cunning Man's Handbook* (2013)

Ed. Ash William Mills

The Unpropitious days, *Some Observations on Egyptian Calendars of lucky and Unlucky Days*, **Warren R. Dawson (1926)**

January 1st and 25th

February 4th and 26th

March 1st and 28th

April 10th and 20th

May 3rd and 25th

June 10th and 16th

July 13th and 22nd

August 1st and 30th

September 3rd and 21st

October 3rd and 22nd

November 5th and 28th

December 7th and 22nd

Chapter 4: Divination Part I, *The Cunning Man's Handbook* (2013)

Recommended reading

Fifty-four Devils: The Art & Folklore of Fortune-telling with Playing Cards (2013) by Cory Thomas Hutcheson

Tea Leaves, Herbs and Flowers: Fortune-telling the Gypsy Way (1998) by Gillian Kemp

The Fortune-Telling Book: Reading Crystal Balls, Tea Leaves, Playing Cards, and Everyday Omens of Love and Luck (2000) by Gillian Kemp

Witchcraft & Second Sight in the Highlands & Islands of Scotland (1902) by John Gregorson Campbell

The Cunning Man's Handbook by Jim Baker

Primitive Beliefs in the Northeast of Scotland (1929) by J.M. McPherson

Reading Cards, Throwing Bone, and Other Forms of Household Fortune-telling (2013) by Mama Starr Casas

Online Sources:

OMNIA: Has a good collection of online digital fortune-telling chapbooks- https://www.omnia.ie/

The National Library of Scotland: Has a few online digital books and chapbooks- https://digital.nls.uk/gallery/

Internet Sacred Texts Archive: Has a large collection of digital grimoires and magic books- https://www.sacred-texts.com/

The Internet Archive: also has a large collection of online and digital material- https://archive.org/

Wikisource- Has archived material of All content with both illustrations of the original book and transcripts https://en.m.wikisource.org/

Printed in Great Britain
by Amazon

36122686R00089